About the Author

Andy Graham was born in Dartford (in Kent) and now lives in East Sussex. He graduated from the University of the West of England and has worked since graduating within the field of data and information management. He has held a number of senior data roles for companies such as Rentokil Initial, HSBC, IMS Health, Sybase, Hummingbird (formally Andyne) and Business Objects.

Writing has become an interest that complements his day to day working life. This book is his fourth following his last book 'A Brief History of Data'. Prior to these two books Andy has published a number of more technical books aimed at data professionals rather that the general public.

You can follow the author via his website at www.andygrahambooks.com

Also by Andy Graham

The Enterprise Data Model: A framework for enterprise data architecture, 2nd edition, published 7th May 2012

Mastering Your Data, published 2015

A Brief History of Data, published 2024

Data Behaving Badly

How data is flawed, fickle and unreliable.

By Andy Graham

Published by Koios Publishing

ISBN: 978-0-9565829-4-2

Printed in the United States of America and the United Kingdom

Typeset in Georgia Pro

To Angela my princess.

Table of Contents

Introduction

The massive internet operation that is Amazon, opened its virtual doors to the public in July 1995. The company had in fact been officially founded a year earlier on the 5th July 1994, under the name "Cadabra" (as in abracadabra). But, within just a few months the name was switched to Amazon Inc because of Cadabra's unpleasant similarity to the word "cadaver". [1] Approximately a year later, the Amazon website was officially published as an online bookseller delivering to all 50 US states and 45 countries globally.

Allegedly the first book ever sold on the site was Douglas Hofstadter's 'Fluid Concepts and Creative Analogies: Computer Models of the Fundamental Mechanisms of Thought'. [2] Within just a few months of opening its doors sales were up to a staggering $20,000 per week. [3] In these early days, Princeton graduate Jeff Bezos was operating the business from the garage of his rented home in Bellevue, Washington. By the end of 2012 the company had grown to employ 88,400 full-time and part-time staff. Over the next 3 years the company grew its workforce by approximately 260% to a figure of 230,800 in December of 2015. [4]

During this tremendous period of growth, the pressure on the recruitment function within Amazon must have been immense. It is unsurprising that by 2014 the recruitment team had started to invest in machine learning programmes to help them wade through the vast lists of candidate CVs they had received for their numerous software development vacancies. The solution to their 'mountain of CV's' problem (metaphorically speaking as most would have been in all likelihood digital), appeared to be an Artificial Intelligence candidate profile rating system. In effect they had created a program that reviewed each applicant's CV's and rate it on a score of 1 to 5, not surprisingly, just like you might rate something you've brought on Amazons own website. This enabled the recruitment team to rapidly sieve through the 100s of candidate CVs to find the top talent. You can imagine the draw of the vision they had created, where the AI technology would propose the best candidate and they would, in this idealistic world, just go ahead and hire them. For a while this worked well until about a year later, in 2015, it started to dawned on hiring departments that they only seem to be hiring male software developers. [5]

So, what went wrong? Whilst the technology had done exactly what it had been asked to do, the whole process was undermined by bias. At that time the technology industry was dominated by men and this inbuilt bias had skewed the AI's results. The machine learning algorithm had been fed the resumes of previously successful applicants from the last 10-year and due to the forementioned male bias it should come as no surprise that the AI had recognised that the majority of successful candidates were male. The software had taught itself that male candidates where better prospects than women (as women hadn't typically applied) and to weed out CV's that included any reference to a female gender, such as all women colleges or clubs.

This story is a great example of how data can cause incorrect, or unexpected, outcomes due to the short fallings inherent in the data. The AI was trained on data that was technically correct but structurally biased. With female candidates significantly underrepresented in the original dataset, the system was never positioned to recognise, let alone realise, the value of diversity. The data used was correct in and of itself, but the data was giving Amazon a skewed view of the world and in effect providing the recruitment team with an untrue representation of the candidate pool they were looking to recruit from.

22 years earlier in 1993, NASA launched its Mars Surveyor program. This endeavour comprised a series of missions in which spacecraft would be used to, as its name suggest, survey the Mars surface. The program was made up of three launches; the first was the Mars Global Surveyor (planned on launching in late 1996), the second was the Mars Climate Orbiter (late 1998) and the final mission was the Mars Polar Lander (early 1999).

The Mars Global Surveyor was launched from Cape Canaveral on the 7th November 1996 on a Delta II rocket and settling into Martian orbit the following year on the 11th September 1997. The space craft spent the next decade examining and mapping Mars.

Introduction

Across its primary mission and multiple extensions, the spacecraft transformed our understanding of Martian geology, climate, and magnetic history. It mapped the planet's topography in unprecedented detail, monitored shifting weather patterns, and revealed the patchwork of remnant magnetic fields locked into the crust. Its instruments also helped identify potential landing sites for future missions, laying the groundwork for rovers like Spirit, Opportunity, Phoenix, and Curiosity.

The second craft, the Mars Climate Orbiter, was launched from the back of a Delta II launch vehicle from Cape Canaveral on the 11th December 1998. Its mission was to study the Martian climate, atmosphere, and surface changes, and to serve as a communications relay for the Mars Polar Lander.

Shortly afterwards, on the 3rd January 1999, the third spacecraft, the Mars Polar Lander, was also launched in the exact same way as the previous orbiter and surveyor. Its objective was to study the soil and climate of the south pole of Mars, including subjects such as the presence of frozen water and carbon dioxide.

On the 23rd September 1999 disaster struck! At 9:04:52 UTC [6] NASA lost contact with the Mars Climate Orbiter.

So, what caused the loss of a $125 million spacecraft after 10 months in space and many years in planning? It seems that there was a mix-up with the units of measurement used within the navigation of the craft. According to the investigation launched by NASA into the incident, the root cause was determined to be a mix-up between metric and imperial measurements. The report states that: '*The MCO MIB has determined that the root cause for the loss of the MCO spacecraft was the failure to use metric units in the coding of a ground software file, "Small Forces," used in trajectory models. Specifically, thruster performance data in English units instead of metric units was used in the software application code titled SM_FORCES (small forces).*'

What had happened was that figures used in the crafts navigation software which was designed to use metric units of Newtonseconds (N-s), instead found itself using imperial units of pounds-seconds (Ibf-s). The spacecraft was intended to skim through Mars' upper atmosphere for several weeks in a technique called aerobraking to reduce velocity and move into a circular orbit. This mistake caused the navigation to go askew, with the spacecrafts flight algorithm giving a trajectory that was out by a factor of 4.45. The Orbiter entering the Martian atmosphere on a dangerously lower than expected trajectory, where it is presumed it broke into pieces and burned up in the planet's atmosphere.

This second story shows how the quality of data can have a devastating impact on those that use it or rely upon the outcomes produced by it. What appears as a ridiculously minor issue, on the surface, in fact had a devastating impact to the Mars Orbiter, ultimately resulting in its demise.

In March 2023 WSB TV, Atlanta Channel 2 Action News had a news item about a local resident, Everett

Tripodis, who had his house demolished by the city of Atlanta authorities. The reason this had made the news was that the destruction of Mr Tripodis's house had been in error. According to the news report he had been sent numerous warnings, but to the wrong address. The property in question is in Lawton Street (zip code 30310) but the letters where being sent to a house in Lawton Avenue (zip code 30314), which is approximately 1.4 miles away. It is alleged that the local authorities had the incorrect address on a number of their internal documents which resulted in this disaster. The whole case is now (at the time of writing) in the hands of lawyers and judges so it's not appropriate to say too much more. [7] Whatever the truth to this story it does go to further reinforce the potential for problems with data to have real world impact.

◇ ◇ ◇

The three stories described in this introduction hopefully give the reader a sense of the impact that bad data can have. Misbehaving data can be devastating but conversely even when the data is perfectly correct it can still have major implications. Accurate information can lead to serious problems when it's misinterpreted, presented poorly, or stripped of the additional context needed to make it make sense.

It's not enough to just refer to data quality because as we have seen perfectly good data if misunderstood can cause just as much of a problem as bad data. What is important is to see the truth in the data. In the English language there is a word for truth -

Introduction

Veracity. The Collins Dictionary defines veracity as 'the quality of being true or the habit of telling the truth'. [8] and the Cambridge University Press describes it as 'the quality of being true, honest, or accurate'. [9] So, we are really looking to understand the veracity of data.

The 'Veracity of Data' has become a common term in the data world of late. We are now capturing data that is not only structured (text and numbers captured in nicely structured computer forms or databases) but also includes unstructured data from the internet, documents, presentation, videos and audio files. Data veracity in this context refers to the reliability of the data, including issues such as bias, noise, abnormalities, incompleteness, errors, outliers, and missing values.

So, what is this book really about? At its core, it's about the uncomfortable truth that data doesn't always tell us the truth. For years, experts have described data as 'the worlds new oil', a resource that will power the global economy of the future. It is true that in today's economy, data fuels innovation, shapes decisions, and drives competitive advantage. Yet unlike oil, it is infinitely replicable, constantly generated, and disturbingly easy to contaminate. The scale is almost unimaginable: in 2022 alone, humanity created, captured, copied, and consumed 97 zettabytes of data, with projections suggesting that number will surge to 181 zettabytes by 2025. So, whilst there is merit in the oil analogy a more fitting comparison, I would argue is data as a form of atomic energy. When handled with care and respect, it can illuminate and empower. When neglected or misunderstood, it can cause serious and far-reaching damage.

1. Fat Fingers

The famous English poet and satirist Alexander Pope wrote the poem 'An Essay on Criticism' in 1711, in which he made the statement, "Good nature and good sense must ever join; to err is human, to forgive divine." [1] [2] Whilst Pope's famous phrase is clearly not about data, his words do have some relevance with the modern world of data and data processing. It is a fact of life that human beings make mistakes. The act of typing data into a computer creates an open invitation for your fingers to freestyle their own creative entries. It's so easy for someone to type an incorrect character, enter a number twice, spell a word incorrectly, use an abbreviation for something instead of the full words, mis-select from a drop-down list, etc. In the final story of this book's introduction chapter (which presumable you've just read), we explored the consequences of an incorrect address being typed into the Atlanta city authority's property records.

In the stockbroking world they even have a phrase for miskeying numbers into brokerage systems – 'fat fingers. For example, on Monday 2nd May 2022 US banking titan City Group issued a statement which said "*This morning one of our traders made an error when inputting a transaction. Within minutes, we identified the error and corrected it*". The simple act of mistyping caused, in this case, a flash crash which is a rapid fall in a single or multiple financial assets prices. Our fat fingered trader caused serval markets to halt trade as they saw indexes plunge. The Nordic market was hit the hardest with Sweden's OMX 30 index dropping 8% before eventually recovering most of that lose to end the day only 1.87% down. [3]

On the 6th April 2018 an employee of Samsung Securities, who was setting up a dividend payout to employees as part of a stock ownership plan, mistyped the units. Instead of entering the currency to be used, which in this case was 'Won', they entered 'Shares'. This meant that 1,000 shares per share were issued as a dividend instead of 1,000 Won being paid out. This simple mis-click resulted in approximately $100 billion worth of shares being distributed to employees rather than the circa $2 billion that was mean to be handed out.

It took Samsung Securities only 37 minutes to realise its error and put a stop on its employees selling any of the incorrected allocation shares. Within that short period of time 16 employees had managed to sell their shares and, in the process make a mint. In total 5 million shares were sold within the 37 minutes before the brakes got applied, which resulted in approximately $187 million being earned. [4]

The fallout from this simple mistype of a key or click of a mouse were huge. The share price of Samsung

Securities plummeted by 11 percent within a day, resulting in the company losing approximately $300 million of its market value. The Korean financial regulator (The Financial Supervisory Service) was concerned that the incident undermined the trust in the countries capital market.

It wasn't only the share price that took a hit. Major customers started to go cold on the company as concerns were raised around a lack of controls; "We have suspended direct trading with Samsung Securities on concerns over decreasing stability in trading after a financial accident occurred," an official with the National Pension Service said. [5]

On the 7th May 2018, Samsung Securities issued statements to the effect that it would look to impose criminal proceeding against the individuals involved. Over the course of the next few years court cases were heard in the Seoul Southern District Court which issued a number of suspended sentences of between 18 months to 2 years with fines imposed as well ranging from 10 to 20 million won (approximately $8-17,000). [6]

On the 28th May the company's headquarters were was raided by South Korean law enforcement officers. [7] [8] Investigators searched the corporate head office in Seocho along with four other premises, looking for evidence of criminal activities.

After examining the evidence collected the regulator handed down a six-month suspension on Samsung Securities onboarding new customers. Additionally, the CEO was suspended from his duties for a three-month period. This was clearly too much as on Friday the 27th July the companies Chief Executive Officer Koo Sung-hoon resigned. [9]

You would think that these stories are rare in the modern financial services industry, but alas even with the huge amount of technology and intellect focused on this part of the global economy these 'fat finger' occurrences aren't as rare as you might think.

Overnight on Wednesday 1st October 2014, the Japan's stock market was overrun with accidental stock orders worth $711 billion. Trades for 42 companies totalling 67.78 trillion yen were mysteriously entered and then equally mysteriously cancelled, all by an anonymous broker. To put this error in perspective, the combined value of the trades was on par with the US government bailout of its banking system during the Global Financial Crisis in 2008. It was also the size of many medium size economies, for example in 2014, the Swedish economy had a Gross Domestic Product (GDP) of approximately $577.73 billion USD. This placed Sweden as the 21st largest economy globally at the time. [10] [11] Luckily, according to a Bloomberg report, all the transactions where voided before they could be executed.

In 2009, we have an employee at UBS Japan accidentally ordered 30 trillion yen worth of debt from Capcom, instead of the intended 30 million yen. In August 2012, Knight Capital caused a major US stock market disruption, costing the company around $440m. A flash crash on the Singapore Exchange in October 2013 saw $6.9 billion in capitalisation wiped out. In the resulting aftermath from this incident, regulators announced new regulations in the following year. [12]

◇ ◇ ◇

Unsurprisingly, this Fat Finger syndrome is not just restricted to the finance industry. In 2003, Spain started to design a new fast attack sub to replace its aging fleet. Its existing subs had been built during the height of the Cold War, and had entered service back in 1977. Their fleet was starting to look dated and it was time for a new generation of crafts. The first of this new generation of subs was the "Isaac Peral", named after the designer of the original electric powered submarine back in 1888. This new submersible was considered so advanced that it could outperform craft built 2 decades later.

Economic headwinds shadowed the development of the Isaac Peral, stretching the project into a decade long delay. During this time, it was discovered that the sub was going to be approximately 100 tons overweight. Now the submersible was expected to be 2,200 tons when floating and 2,430 when submerged so 100 tons doesn't seem like a lot. [13] But at this weight the sub, once submerged, would probably never make it back to the surface. A bit of a critical issue I would think.

It turned out that during the original design there had been a decimal point error which had resulted in the excessive weight gain. After reviewing their options, and probably after a few sangrias to recover from the shock, the engineers decided to extend the length of the boat by 30 feet and add a pressure ring to support this new length. So, the new sub would be a little heavier and a little longer than originally specified, cost nearly double its original budget but that should be ok, shouldn't it? Alas this was not the case!

In 2018 the Spanish government realised that the new size for the craft meant that the port of Cartagena (where it was currently being built) was too small to accommodate it. They had to expand the port to avoid any problems, at an extra cost of $18.6 million. The submarine was eventually christened in 2021, fully able to both fit in the port and surface when required. [14]

The impact of human error on data can have far more series effects than just costing a lot of money. In its 2007 report the US Institute of Medicine estimated that there were 1.5 million medication errors that caused harm to a patient each year. It further estimated that approximately 8,000 patients died each year due to these medication mistakes.

Medication dosage mistakes are quite common it seems and unfortunately often go unnoticed. Mistakes can have significant health impacts. Confusion over units of measure used can cause incorrect dosage to be prescribed. When handed to the pharmacy they will go ahead and issue the drugs not realising that the dosage could be three or four times higher than the intended dose.

There are several cases where incorrect dosages for paediatric patients have resulted in serious injury or death. Swapping pounds and kilograms, or even just having the wrong weight to begin with, can make a serious impact on a patient. [15] [16] [17]

Data discrepancies caused by incorrectly entered or captured information, whether typed into a computer system, written on a paper form, or collected through any other method, are far more common than we realise. As we've seen, they can lead to serious problems, costing money, wasting time, and even affecting people's health. On a more mundane level these impacts can cause businesses to struggle to connect to customers because the details they captured about the customer or prospect were incorrect. It's difficult for digital marketing folk to run effective email campaigns when the data captured in their corporate systems is inaccurate. Missing key elements such as the email domain or the presence of information that doesn't belong in the email field, like internal notes, can prevent messages from being sent at all.

What about a sales person looking to capture the name of another contact, or a second phone number for the contact, at a company but the CRM system he is using only allows one name or one phone number. If the system allows it (and doesn't have validation in place to prevent) he will type the extra name or phone number into the field intended for just the one.

◇ ◇ ◇

To end this chapter on a more light hearted note, some data typos can create more interesting outcomes. Take as an example the naming of the search engine 'Google'. The story goes that back in 1996 when the original inventors of Google (Larry

Page and Sergey Brin) where naming their new search engine they had actually landed on the name 'BackRub'. As BackRub grew the pair started to look for a new name to better represent the scale of the product. A fellow student by the name of Sean Anderson suggested the name 'googolplex' which got shortened by Page to 'googol' which represents the mathematical expression for the number 1 followed by 100 zeros. Allegedly at this stage when checking the availability for the web domain google was typed in by mistake. The name seems to have stuck, hence in 1997 the web domain 'google.com' was registered and the rest is history. [18]

The Wicked Bible, also known as the Adulterous Bible or Sinners' Bible, is a rare 1631 edition of the Bible. It is called "wicked" because it omitted the word "not" from the seventh commandment, making it read "thou shalt commit adultery". Only one thousand copies of this Bible were originally printed, and the error was noticed a year later. [19] [20]

2. Square Peg, Round Hole

The French Foreign Minister Robert Schuman proposed the integration of the coal and steel industries of Western Europe which would restrict the ability of any single country making the weapons needed for war. In 1952 Germany, France, Italy, the Netherlands, Belgium and Luxembourg formed the European Coal and Steel Community. Five years later building upon the success of the Coal and Steel Treaty, the 6 founding countries expand their cooperation and signed the Treaties of Rome. This created the European Economic Community (EEC) which aimed to foster economic integration among its member states. Over the years, the EEC evolved into the European Community (EC) and eventually the EU, which was formalised by the Maastricht Treaty in 1992.

One of the driving forces behind this steady integration has been the intent for countries to work together on collaborations for the benefit of the whole European community. One of the early attempts at undertaking such a project came about with the development of the 'Airbus'. The Airbus project was born in July 1967 when a joint statement from French, German and British ministers stated *"for the purpose of strengthening European co-operation in the field of aviation technology and thereby promoting economic and technological progress in Europe, to take appropriate measures for the joint development and production of an airbus."* Behind this statement was the recognitions by government ministers that something needed to be done to protect the European aviation industry from being dominated by the Americans.

Since the end of the second world war the European aviation industry had remained highly nationalistic. Dozens of smaller European plane makers were spread across France, Germany, and the United Kingdom. In France we have the Caravelle and the Sud Aviation's Galion. In the UK we had the Comet, the BAC1-11 and the Trident. It was becoming clear that whilst there was huge innovation coming out of Europe the fragmented nature of the aviation industry at that time meant Europe would struggle to compete against the monopoly that the North American companies such as Boeing, Douglas, and Lockheed had. The market was just too small.

Whilst Europe had introduced the world to jet travel by the 1960 it was the US that was making 80% of the world's aircraft. The fractional nature of the European market with companies and nations competing against each other meant that the US had been able to take approximately 80% of the world's aviation market. To help put this into context, Boeings first airliner, the 707, sold 1,010 planes whilst its most popular European competitor, the Sud-Aviation Caravelle, only racked up 277 sales.

If Europe didn't respond then huge numbers of jobs would be at risk and the proud European aircraft industry would be demoted to parts manufacturers for American aircraft industry. By combining the skills and talents that existed within the combined European market into a single organisation and therefore a series of European aircraft, they would be able to standup to the dominate Americans. Thus, in September 1967, France, Germany, and the United Kingdom signed a memorandum of understanding to kick-off the A300 project. The A300 was a short to medium haul twin engine widebody plane, a world's first. The A300 was a groundbreaking design, offering a widebody cabin with only two engines, making it more fuel-efficient than its three-engine competitors like the McDonnell Douglas DC-10 and Lockheed L-1011 TriStar.

The goal of this initiative was simple: to pool the industrial capacity and areas of excellence offered by each country. French engineer, Roger Béteille, who was appointed technical director of the A300 programme said *"I wanted to use all the available talents and capacities to their utmost without worrying about the colour of the flag or what language was spoken"* [1] [2]. France was to be in charge of building the cockpit, flight controls, and the lower centre section of the fuselage. The Germans would make the forward and rear fuselage sections, plus the upper part of the centre section, and the United Kingdom would take care of the wings and the engines. Eventually this endeavour was joined by the

Dutch (making the moving parts of the wing such as flaps and spoilers) and the Spanish (who would build the horizontal tailplane).

In 2000 Airbus started work on the infamous A380, the largest commercial passenger aircraft ever flown, with a maximum capacity of 853 passengers. The plane was conceived as Airbus's long-haul answer to Boeings 747. Whilst the advantage Airbus had over its competition was the ability to leverage the skills and talents of many different countries this was also its Achillies heel. What began as an ambitious, continent spanning collaboration slowly turned into a nightmare as the project stretched on for more than fifteen years, slipping roughly four years beyond the original plan. The first plane was due to be delivered in 2006. Six years to the uninitiated seems like a long time but for a program like the A380 project it's not. In April 2005 the first test flight took place but by this time it had become evident that the Airbus project was being impacted by a series of IT problems. Shortly afterwords, the manufacturer announced a series of delays.

So, what went wrong? Each country, whilst diligently working on their part of the aircraft, worked in a silo just as they always had. They had different systems, different data formats, different processes and spectacularly failed to communicate with each other about changes to plans and designs. For example, the Germans where using an old version of a design software product called CATIA to design the miles of wiring required for the aircraft's wings. The French on the other hand whilst using the same software product had a much later version which they used to design the wing structures that the wiring needed to fit.

To get a sense of the scale of the problem, just consider that an A380 has about 100,000 different wires that measured approximately 530 kilometres in length, if layer out in a continuous line, and about 40,000 connectors. [3] However, after spending weeks weaving through the electrical wiring, the engineers and mechanics realised that the wiring was too short. *"The wiring wasn't following the expected routing through the fuselage, so when we got to the end, they weren't long enough to meet up with the connectors on the next section"* reported Simple Fly quoting a final assembly mechanic. It was reported in the New York Times that they were told by an employee that *"Everything had to be ripped out and replaced from scratch"*. [4] [5]

Ultimately, the two different versions of CATIA simply couldn't talk to each other. Designs that should have passed seamlessly between teams failed, forcing Airbus into an enormously expensive redesign. German engineers tried to bridge the gap with custom file-conversion tools, but even this wasn't possible. The misalignment is estimated to have cost around $6 billion in corrective work and delayed the aircraft's delivery by two years. This meant that launch customer Singapore Airlines wasn't able to carry their first fare-paying passengers on an A380 until October 2007.

The company acknowledged the initial production delay just a month after the aircraft's maiden flight, and a year later it was forced to announce yet another six-to-seven-month setback. Not surprisingly investor confidence evaporated with Airbus's share price plummeting.

For a programme that ultimately burned through more than $6 billion because two software systems couldn't communicate due to data formatting issues, the A380's troubles stand as a stark reminder of how a simple breakdown in coordination can unravel even the most ambitious engineering vision.

◇ ◇ ◇

Technology is complex and is one of the most pedantic creatures in the world. Any time you move data from one system to another, things can go wrong. It doesn't matter whether it's a big one-off migration or the everyday transfer of information between systems, there are always plenty of chances for problems to creep in. Technology can be a little like a child trying to put a square peg in the round hole in their toy. Bashing it harder just doesn't work. In the case of computers trying to talk to other computers either the data doesn't get transferred or it does but data gets all mixed up as the data goes into the wrong bucket. In effect the wires have been wired up incorrectly. The results can be quite devastating.

◇ ◇ ◇

Its early morning on the 4th June, 1996, at Kourou in the French overseas department of French Guiana, which is located on the northern coast of South America. The weather had been stormy overnight but had calmed down enough that the maiden flight of the European latest space rocket the Ariane 5 could go ahead. It had been rainy but the conditions had improved and the risk of lightning was considered low due to the strength of the electric field measured at the launch site being negligible. At 9:33:59s local time (12:33:59s UT) the Vulcain engine and the two solid boosters where ignited and lift-off occurred.

The rocket launched as expected until 37 seconds into the flight when it suddenly veered off its flight path, broke up, and exploded. The destruction of the Ariane 5 occurred about 1 km away from the launch pad and at an altitude of approximately 4 km. The resulting debris was scattered across 12 km^2 area of mangrove swamps and savanna. Not only did the terrain make it difficult to recover the wreckage but poisonous substances, from the spacecraft, rained down on the crash site; causing the surrounding area to be evacuated. [6]

The European Space Agency's official report into the Ariane flight failure, written by Chair of the Board Prof. J. L. LIONS concluded that the rocket disintegrated because of an angle of attack of more than 20 degrees. This led to a higher than expected aerodynamic load which in turn caused the separation of the boosters from the main stage which ultimately caused the rockets destruct. The report goes on to say:

This angle of attack was caused by full nozzle deflections of the solid boosters and the Vulcain main engine.

These nozzle deflections were instigated by the On-Board Computer (OBC) software on the basis of data transmitted by the active Inertial Reference System

(SRI 2). This, it seems, was caused by inaccurate flight data being transmitted between the SRI 2 and the OBC. In fact, what was transmitted was not flight data at all but diagnostic data and this was dually interpreted as flight data.

The reason why the active SRI 2 did not send correct attitude data was that the unit had declared a failure due to a software exception. The OBC could not switch to the back-up SRI 1 because that unit had already ceased to function during the previous data cycle (72 milliseconds period) for the same reason as SRI 2.

"The internal SRI software exception was caused during execution of a data conversion from 64-bit floating point to 16-bit signed integer value. The floating point number which was converted had a value greater than what could be represented by a 16-bit signed integer. This resulted in an Operand Error. The data conversion instructions (in Ada code) were not protected from causing an Operand Error, although other conversions of comparable variables in the same place in the code were protected."

The section of the report I've outlined above is the key issue that caused all this destruction. In essence one computer program tried to take a number represented in a very specific mathematical format and precision and stuff it into a different computer program that was expected a completely different format of number and hence computer said no and the destruction we have already outlined above occurred. Try to imagine a computer program trying to stuff the proverbial square peg in the round hole of a second computer program.

The estimated development cost of the Ariane 5 was somewhere in the region of $8bn (£4bn). On board the rocket where some scientific equipment that was meant to be carried into space to study how the Earth's magnetic field interacts with Solar Winds. This payload was estimated to be worth an additional $500 million (£240 million).

◇ ◇ ◇

As the clock struck midnight on the 31st December 1999, billions of people around the world celebrated the new millennium as we entered the year 2000. For those partying, this would be a unique experience that they will never again witness. In Australia millions watched, in person, one of the most spectacular fireworks displays, 2000 doves of peace were released in Bethlehem, four tonnes of confetti was dropped on the heads of the three million people in Times Square, New York. In the Scottish city of Edinburgh, where the largest Hogmanay celebration ever was underway, an estimated five tonnes of fireworks were fired into the night sky over the course of just four minutes. [7]

Whilst all this excitement was going on, another event didn't occur. Yes, you read that correctly. The event we are talking about is the feared worldwide computer meltdown that was caused by the Millennium Bug. The fear was so real that the United States government passed into law the 'Year 2000 Information and Readiness Disclosure Act'. It also monitored the preparedness of private companies.

Whilst it's impossible to know the true cost of fixing/preparing for this event, according to the research company Gartner the cost for fixing the Y2K bug has been estimated to be between $300 billion to $600 billion. [8]

Planes didn't fall out of the sky, banking systems didn't fail and you could therefore still get money from the bank cash dispensers. In effect everything carried on as normal. I've included this non disaster story in this chapter as, although it all went swimmingly in the end, the huge amount of time and money that was invested in the prevention of the disaster demonstrates the business impact, of a relatively small data format mistake in a vast number of IT systems.

U.S. businesses and government agencies are being forced to spend about $100 billion to keep the year 2000 glitch from crashing their computers, making a simple two-digit programming "bug" the most expensive peacetime catastrophe in modern history. [9]

So, what was behind this very expensive non story? In essence computer systems for decades had been developed using just two digits to store the year part of any date. This meant that the year 1976 would be stored as '76' and the year 1999 would be stored as '99'. The problem came about when we reached the year 2000 as the year would be stored as '00'. The concern was that their legacy computer systems would interpret '00' as the year 1900 rather than 2000 and the implication of this mistake could have dramatic impact. Financial companies were worried about interest being calculated on customers account incorrectly or that customers might not be able to withdraw money. Airlines were worried about airline reservation systems not being able to take booking or getting the books wrong. There were even scare stories in the news about the potential of airplanes falling out of the sky.

Many IT vendors and contractors did handsomely out of the billions poured into averting what was billed as the great technological reckoning of the age. Tales of eye-watering day rates and gold-plated retainers circulated freely. Then midnight arrived, time zone by time zone, and the world braced itself for digital Armageddon. What followed was ... nothing. No collapsing systems, no planes falling from the sky, just fireworks and hangovers.

So why dwell on it here? Because the absence of catastrophe is beside the point. The real story isn't the disaster that never came, but the original, quietly calamitous decision to encode dates in two digits and to keep doing so long after it was obviously unwise. The UK House of Commons Library later estimated the cost of fixing that choice at £400 billion.

That is why the Millennium Bug earns its place in this book: not as a tale of doom, but as a reminder of how small data decisions can mature into vast, expensive problems.

3. Misunderstanding the data

On the 3rd August 1492, three ships left the Spanish port of Palos. 71 days later on the morning of the 13th October the leader of this small flotilla, Christopher Columbus, stepped ashore in what he though was Asia. In actual fact he had landed on an island of the Caribbean, which is part of the Americas, thousands of miles away from his actual destination.

The three small ships under Columbus's command (the Niña, Pinta and the Santa María) left Spain and made their way to the Canary Islands, the far edge of Spanish territory and the last touch of land before the unknown. There they were delayed far longer than planned due to a lack of wind. Only on 8 September, after weeks of frustrating calm, were they able to depart and push westward into the deep ocean on what they believed would be their route to China.

According to the calculations Columbus had made in mapping out this epic voyage the trip should take no more than 4 weeks, but after 4 weeks at sea, land was frustratingly absent. 32 days out from the Canaries (12 October) the Piñta spotted land. Whilst the identity of his landfall island is in dispute (it was most likely one of the Plana Cays in the Bahamas) the rest is history. [1]

Columbus, the Genoese son of a weaver and tavern-keeper, emerged from the bustle of 15th-century Italy at a moment when Europe was gripped by a fever for discovery. Born around 1451 in Genoa (Italy), he had taken to the sea in his teenage years due to his father's love of sea travel. [2] This was an era when the great powers of Europe were pouring money into voyages that promised new lands and untold riches The Portuguese had been doing this for years by exploring and exploiting the African continent.

One of the dreamed of parts of the world was the exotic lands of Asia. At this time in history, it was virtually impossible to get there by land from Europe. The Portuguese had found a route by travelling around Africa. The problem was that this required a long and challenging journey and that it was easy for the Portuguese to block that route for other nations.

Columbus had the bright idea of breaking this monopoly on trade by Portugal by travelling directly there by sailing west across the Atlantic. He touted his ideas across Europe and eventually found support in Spain. The deal he struck with the Spanish monarchs, Ferdinand of Aragon and Isabella of Castile, entitled him to 10% of all treasures he discovered along with the governorship of the lands he would conquer/discover.

Contrary to popular belief back in the 15th century it was known that the Earth was not flat, but was actually spherical. Whilst not everyone would have subscribed to this view, it had in fact been known for centuries. It was the Greek scholar Eratosthenes who first calculated the circumference of the earth, way back in the third century BC. The historian Jeffrey Burton Russell, concluded that "no educated person in the history of Western civilisation from the 3rd century BC onwards believed that the Earth was flat". [3]

Modern engineering student are taught from day one to 'watch your units!' Keeping the units of measure being used consistent by converting where needed, is important in preventing errors in calculations. This is exactly what went wrong with Columbus.

The famous 9th century Arabic astronomer Alfraganus (800 – 870 BC), composed several works on astronomy including his own calculation for the Earths circumference. His works were widely distributed in Arabic and Latin and influenced Christopher in his calculations for his voyages to America.

Columbus studied both these scholars work but ultimately settled on Alfraganus's version. This was fine except he seems to not realise, or forget, that the former was measured in roman miles and the later in Arabic miles. Working under the incorrect assumption that Alfraganua's calculations were based upon Roman miles meant that his calculations where approximately 25% out. A Roman mile is 4,856 feet long whilst an Arabic mile was 7,091 feet. He also got the location of Japan wrong. All of these mistakes resulted in Columbuses calculations being out by 58% in his estimate of the distance from Europe to the East Indies. [4]

Chapter 3

The story of Christopher Columbus's discovery of the Americas is a story of how misinterpretation of data lead to unexpected outcomes. In this case the result changed history in ways Columbus could not have ever imagined.

◇ ◇ ◇

In Georgina Sturge's fantastic book "Bad Data" she explains, based upon her experience as a UK government statistician, how statistics can be badly used and misunderstood. For example, she tells the story of how the 2011 census found that there were approximately half a million more people living in the United Kingdom that had been thought to reside in the country.

Now migration has been a hot potato in UK politics for decades, but it's only in the past 20-30 years that it has become the defining fault line of national debate. The early skirmishes of the 1960s and 70s with Enoc Powell's River of Bloods speech and the first immigration acts were really just the introduction. The real story begins in the 1990s, when asylum numbers rose, the tabloids found a new obsession, and Westminster discovered that immigration could move votes. Then came the noughties and the EU free movement and especially the impact of the 2004 enlargement which put a rocket under the migration issue. By the 2010s, immigration wasn't merely an issue, it had become 'the' issue. Impacting elections and referendums

With that backdrop in mind, the 'extra' residents uncovered by the 2011 census turned out to be migrants. But how had this happened? How had this happened? The standard method used to estimate the population was to take the number of births, subtracting deaths, and then adjust for people entering and leaving the country. On the surface, it all seemed perfectly until you dig into how the last part was actually arrived at.

The numbers had baffled and embarrassed government statisticians because, as mentioned above, they had spent years surveying travellers entering and leaving the country. The problem lay in the International Passenger Survey, which had been running since 1961 as was the main tool used to estimate migration. It operated across the main ports and airports, yet somehow failed to detect the surge in migration.

The statisticians had assumed that most people would arrive through major hubs such as Heathrow or Gatwick. In doing so, they largely overlooked the growing traffic through smaller regional airports — Luton, Leeds, and others — on the basis that the volumes would be negligible. But with the expansion of the EU, the opening of the UK's borders to the eight new accession countries (Czech Republic, Estonia, Hungary, Latvia, Lithuania, Poland, Slovakia and Slovenia) and the rapid rise of budget airlines flying into those regional airports, a huge cohort of migrants simply slipped past the survey's field of vision. [5]

◇ ◇ ◇

In July 1983 we have the first successful emergency "dead stick" landing of a commercial jetliner in an Air Canada Boeing 767. The pilots of the Ottawa-to-Edmonton flight had lost power to both engines and had to make an emergency landing. The landing was an exciting affair with the pilots being unable to slow the planes speed using the flaps, due to the engine failure, and therefore they approached the runway at Gimli, Manitoba, at about 180 knots which is 40 knots over the typical landing speed. Luckily there wasn't any serious damage; the plane's nose gear collapsed, and two passengers suffered minor injuries.

It's hard not to marvel at the sheer Canadian understatement of it all. A Boeing 767, robbed of power by a metric mix-up, gliding towards what should have been a very final full stop and yet the captain, Robert Pearson, treated the whole affair rather as if he were coaxing a sailplane into a summer thermic. Ten years of glider flying will do that to a man. Then there was the copilot, Maurice Quintal, who happened to know the abandoned Gimli airfield from his Air Force days. The place had long since been handed over to drag-racers and weekend thrill-seekers. The result was a landing that had more thrills that the airfield had seen for year.

It seems that in all this excitement the plane had actually run out of fuel, and this was down to a change from imperial to metric. Now fuel is a complex topic when it comes to airplanes, as they only carry the fuel needed to complete the flight in question (obviously with an appropriate safety margin). Carrying too much fuel would mean unnecessary weight and higher consumption of costly fuel.

Due to problems with the planes electronic gauging system the fuel had to be measured manually, using those quaintly named "drip sticks". For years Air

Canada, had been measured fuel weight in pounds and that's what happened on the carriers first metric aircraft. What the pilots believed was a healthy fuel load in kilograms was, in fact, a far more meagre quantity measured in pounds. Given that a kilogram outweighs a pound by a factor of 2.2, the aircraft left the gate with barely half the fuel it needed. [6]

4. Lies, Dam Lies and Statistics

"There are three kinds of lies: lies, damned lies, and statistics." [1]

There is a fantastic sketch that played out in the BBC TV series Yes, Prime Minister that captures the dark art of shaping opinion better than any modern political guru. In the episode "The Ministerial Broadcast," (Series 1, Episode 2) which was originally aired in 1986, we find Sir Humphrey Appleby delivering a masterclass to his colleague Bernard Woolley, revealing how a survey's outcome can be engineered long before a single member of the public is consulted. With careful phrasing and rearranging of questions, he shows how "public opinion" can be coaxed, nudged, or outright marched toward whatever conclusion the government of the day finds most convenient. [2]

Sir Humphrey Appleby:	*Mr. Woolley, are you worried about the rise in crime among teenagers?*

Bernard Woolley:	*Yes*
Sir Humphrey Appleby:	*Do you think there is lack of discipline and vigorous training in our Comprehensive Schools?*
Bernard Woolley:	*Yes.*
Sir Humphrey Appleby:	*Do you think young people welcome some structure and leadership in their lives?*
Bernard Woolley:	*Yes.*
Sir Humphrey Appleby:	*Do they respond to a challenge?*
Bernard Woolley:	*Yes.*
Sir Humphrey Appleby:	*Might you be in favour of reintroducing National Service?*
Bernard Woolley:	*Er, I might be.*
Sir Humphrey Appleby:	*Yes or no?*
Bernard Woolley:	*Yes.*
Sir Humphrey Appleby:	*Of course, after all you've said you can't say no to that. On the other hand, the*

surveys can reach opposite conclusions. [survey two] Mr. Woolley, are you worried about the danger of war?

Bernard Woolley:	*Yes.*
Sir Humphrey Appleby:	*Are you unhappy about the growth of armaments?*
Bernard Woolley:	*Yes.*
Sir Humphrey Appleby:	*Do you think there's a danger in giving young people guns and teaching them how to kill?*
Bernard Woolley:	*Yes.*
Sir Humphrey Appleby:	*Do you think it's wrong to force people to take arms against their will?*
Bernard Woolley:	*Yes.*
Sir Humphrey Appleby:	*Would you oppose the reintroduction of conscription?*
Bernard Woolley:	*Yes.* *[does a double-take]*
Sir Humphrey Appleby:	*There you are, Bernard. The perfectly balanced sample.*

The sketch is a fantastic illustration of how by asking a series of leading questions, one can elicit contradictory responses on the same issue - in this case, the reintroduction of national service. The relevance of this ability to manipulate results was demonstrated many years later by Ipsos; the multinational market research and consulting firm. They undertook a real-world experiment by asking two separate groups of 1,000 people two different sets of questions about national service. As in the Yes Prime Minister sketch one group had a set of questions that were positive about the idea and the second group had the negative questions.

The Positive Questionnaire asked the following questions:

- Question1 - Are you worried about the number of young people without jobs?
- Question 2 - Are you worried about the rise in crime among teenagers?
- Question3 - Do you think there's a lack of discipline in Britain's comprehensive schools?
- Question 4 - Do you think young people would welcome some authority and leadership in their lives?
- Question 5 - Would you be in favour of reintroducing National Service in Britain?

The second group with the negative questions were asked:

- Question 1 - Are you worried about the danger of war?
- Question 2 - Are you worried about the growth of armaments / weapons around the world?

- Question 3 - Do you think there's a danger in giving young people guns and teaching them how to kill?
- Question 4 - Do you think it's wrong to force people to take up arms against their will?
- Question 5 - Would you oppose the reintroduction of National Service in Britain?

In the positive group we have a 45% yes vote as opposed to a no vote of 38% and with the negative group a similar result with 48% of the group against national service and only 34% for it. From the results it is clear that the way you frame a question will impact on your answer. [3]

◊ ◊ ◊

If we go back in time to the father of data science, John Graunt, we find the first references to data issues with statistics and how they were being manipulated. Although a haberdasher by trade his interest in science and numbers led him to focus his attention on the 'Bills of Mortality' that were published weekly for each London Parish. He concluded that by compiling the data together over many issues a huge amount could be learned. [4]

The Bills of Mortality were originally started to monitor plague deaths in the late 15th century and continued on until the 19th century. It eventually expanded beyond just plague deaths to include baptisms and death by any cause. In 1662 he published the snappily titled book 'Natural and Political Observations Mentioned in a Following Index, and Made Upon the Bills of Mortality'. This impressively entitled book also had an impressive number of observations.

His book included the first actuarial table (also called a mortality or life table). This is a table showing for any given age group what the probability is that, that person will not survive until their next birthday. This probability of death calculation is fundamental to today's life insurance industry.

Graunt identified that plague deaths were being under recorded because, in years where there was a rise in plague deaths, he could also see that more deaths for other reasons had occurred. He estimated that 20% of plague deaths were recorded incorrectly. Whilst this allowed him to refine his estimates it was also the first known example of data quality remediation.

Graunt also called out that data quality issues caused by bribery where under reporting the cases of syphilis, or as it was known at the time the 'French-Pox'. If left untreated syphilis can be fatal so Graunt was surprised that of the 229,250 deaths in the period he was studying at the time he only had 392 deaths by the French-Pox recorded. As "*a great part of men have, at one time, or other, had some species of this disease*", it seemed fanciful that the numbers would be so low to Graunt.

It turned out that most of the syphilis deaths were being recorded as consumption. He reported that a two-groat bribe was behind his data inaccuracy. "*the Old-women Searchers after the mist of a Cup of Ale, and the bribe of a two-groat fee, instead of one, given them, cannot tell whether this emaciation, or leanness were from a Phthisis, or from an Hectick Fever, Atrophy, &c. or from an Infection of the Spermatick parts"*. [4] [5]

The Literary Digest, a widely read magazine in the US, launched in October 1936 a poll to assess public opinion on the up and coming presidential election in November of the same year. As the election approached, the magazine mailed out ten million ballots to citizens across the United States. It was a mammoth effort as each day, more than a quarter of a million envelopes were addressed by hand. The mailing list was compiled from telephone directories, club rosters, city registers, voter rolls, and mail order records, all in an attempt to capture the voice of the nation.

The response rate was approximately 24% which was seen at the time as a reliable cross-section of the electorate. It predicted that the Republican candidate, Alfred Landon, would win the election with 54% of the vote with an estimated 370 electoral votes out of 531. The actual result was as predicted a landslide but not in the way that The Literary Digest expected. In fact, the landslide was far more decisive that predicted at 523 electoral votes vs 8. The biggest shock though was that the Democratic candidate Franklin D. Roosevelt won with over 60% of the popular vote. He managed to carry every state except Maine and Vermont. The Digest's forecast was not just wrong; it was spectacularly wrong.

So how did they get this so wrong with such a large number of respondents? The answer to that question has become a textbook example of how not to run a poll. Although they had received 2.4 million responses the data contained bias which screwed the results.

The magazine's readership was mostly well-off Americans, the kind of people who owned cars and telephones. It should be remembered that at the time a fixed line telephone was a luxury, with only about 17–20 million landlines across the entire country. This compares to 202w and the contrast in the US is almost comical with more than 372 mobile subscriptions, this equates to approximately 1.1 cell phones per head of population.

So, the demographic of the publication's readership meant the sample leaned heavily toward voters who were already more likely to back Landon, while millions of lower-income Roosevelt supporters were never contacted at all. In today's language, it was a classic case of sample bias. [6] [7]

Secondly, the 2.5 million people that responded would be more likely to be politically engaged and due to the demographic (see above) are more likely to be republican in their political leanings. The Digest had assumed, in error, that the respondents mirrored the broader population. This is called Nonresponse Bias.

The collapse of the Literary Digest poll serves as a powerful reminder that having huge amounts of data does not guarantee better results. By failing to account for the demographic imbalance among survey recipients and neglecting corrective measures such as weighting or stratification the poll fell victim to its own flawed assumptions. Despite collecting millions of responses, its design flaws rendered the results misleading.

In the age of big data, this lesson is more relevant than ever. Without thoughtful sampling and methodological rigor, even vast datasets can amplify bias rather than reveal truth.

Interestingly, the ballot included a question about respondents' voting behaviour in the previous election of 1932. This retrospective data could have been used to weight the responses, and had the pollsters applied such adjustments, they might have mitigated the bias introduced by their sampling strategy and avoided going down in history as one of the most infamous polling mistakes ever. [8] [9]

The Literary Digest story might look like an amusing historical footnote, but the underlying problem is anything but rare. In fact, almost all scientific studies have some missing observations. According to the BMJ (a long-established, globally respected medical journal) 'Almost all studies have some missing observations", yet most textbooks and news stories quietly assume the opposite. It's one of those statistical blind spots that hides in plain sight. [10]

Missingness creeps in through dozens of mundane pathways:

- Postal surveys where a chunk of people never reply
- Randomised trials where patients drift out of follow-up
- Multicentre studies where some sites skip a variable

- High-frequency assessments where time-points simply vanish
- Equipment failures that wipe out individual readings
- Lab samples lost, spoiled, or unusable
- MRI studies excluding participants who don't fit the machine
- Quality-of-life studies where participants die during follow-up

Each mechanism carries its own implications, but the central question never changes: does the missingness introduce bias? A handful of missing observations is an irritation. A large amount is a structural threat to the integrity of the entire study. And because missingness is so ubiquitous, the real risk isn't the gaps themselves, it's pretending they aren't there.

◇ ◇ ◇

There is a great mini-series called 'Dopesick', released in 2021, that tells the story of the OxyContin Marketing scandal. He series had great success with Michael Keaton awarded an Emmy and Golden Globes for his performance of Dr. Samuel Finnix.

The OxyContin scandal started in the late 1990s with Purdue Pharma's launch of a marketing campaign for its new painkiller, OxyContin, that would become a textbook case in how data can be weaponised. Purdue Pharma manufactures pain medicines such as hydromorphone, fentanyl, codeine, hydrocodone and oxycodone, also known by its brand name, OxyContin. The company has been owned since the 50's by the Sackler family but at time of writing was going through Chapter 11 bankruptcy with a new company called Knoa Pharma, planned to emerge from the process.

The OxyContin campaign was not just aggressive, it was deceptive. At the core of the lie was a graph which claimed to show the drug's steady release over 12 hours and its low risk of addiction. The chart was simple, clean, persuasive and it was a lie.

The graph used a logarithmic scale to flatten the curve of drug concentration in the bloodstream, masking the sharp drop-off that patients experienced well before the promised 12-hour mark. Withdrawal symptoms and breakthrough pain were common, but the marketing materials insisted otherwise. The data behind the graph was cherry-picked from short-term studies, ignoring mounting evidence of long-term dependency and abuse. The illusion of safety was not just misleading, it was lethal.

Purdue's sales representatives were trained to repeat the mantra: "less than 1% addiction risk." This figure came from a brief letter to the editor in a medical journal, not a peer-reviewed study. It was cited as gospel. Doctors were bombarded with promotional videos, glossy brochures, and incentivized visits from reps who earned bonuses for pushing high-dose prescriptions. The company's internal documents later revealed a deliberate strategy to expand OxyContin's use beyond cancer pain to everyday ailments such as backaches, arthritis, post-surgical recovery, etc. All this despite the lack of long-term safety data.

When the FDA finally requested changes to the drug's labelling, Purdue exploited the revisions to reinforce its marketing narrative. The new language was twisted into a selling point, not a warning. Regulatory compromise became a tool for further deception. The results were catastrophic. Within five years, OxyContin was the most prescribed Schedule II narcotic in the United States. Addiction rates soared. Overdose deaths climbed. Entire communities, particularly in Appalachia, were devastated. Purdue Pharma pleaded guilty to felony misbranding in 2007, paying hundreds of millions in fines. But the damage was done.

This case is not just about one company's greed. It is a cautionary tale of how data when stripped of context, distorted by design, and wielded with intent can become a weapon.

5. Fake News

On the morning of Monday 21st February 1814, a man walks into the Ship Inn in Dover, England, and loudly announcing the tremendous news that Napoleon I of France had been killed! At this time half of Europe was at war with France and Napoleons army so this was wonderful news. The uniformed soldier called himself Colonel du Bourg and claiming to be the aide-de-camp to Lord Cathcart. General Charles Murray Cathcart (the 2nd Earl Cathcart) is an interesting character who' was famous for the unfortunate bad luck of having three horses shot from under him at the Battle of Waterloo. [1]

The Colonel asked that the information about Napoleons demise be relayed to the Admiralty in London forthwith via semaphore telegraph. A semaphore telegraph is a series of towers equipped with pivoting arms or blades, which can be positioned in various angles to represent different letters or messages. Operators at each tower would observe the position of the arms on the neighbouring tower through a telescope and relay the message by adjusting their own arms accordingly. This system could convey messages in a fraction of the time it would traditionally take, making it a crucial tool for military and governmental communication. Interesting the technology had been invented by France.

He next travelled to London, stopping at numerous inns on the way to spread the news far and wide. Around the same time a group of three men, in French officers in Bourbon uniforms, were seen celebrating in London proclaiming the restoration of the Bourbon monarchy.

Though Napoleon did, eventually, die, he was still very much alive at the time and would live on until 1821. Napoleon in fact fought on until Paris fell in March of the same year. But the English didn't know that, and the man who bore the news looked legit: He wore a military uniform and acted the part of Colonel du Bourg convincingly. He also gave the locals the juicy details they wanted to hear: "The Allies are in Paris, Bonaparte is dead, destroyed by the Cossacks, and literally torn in a thousand pieces; the Cossacks fought for a share of him as if they were fighting for gold," he said. "The country can expect a speedy peace."

And soon, stocks - which, at the time, looked more like today's bonds - rose. The story was eventually found out by authorities to be a hoax (or as we would call it today 'Fake News'), but not before stockholders were able to make a lot of money selling off their government securities at suddenly very good prices.

Behind the fraud was a group of eight people, including naval hero and Parliament member Lord Cochrane. Six of them were tried and sentenced to a year of prison time and public humiliation. [2]

Hailed by Collins Dictionary as the 2017's word of the year, the phrase captures *"fake, often sensational, information disseminated under the guise of news reporting."* [3] Despite academic unease about its imprecision, "fake news" has evolved into a catch-all label used to describe the spread of misleading or harmful content across today's media environment.

While the phrase "fake news" has only relatively recently entered everyday vocabulary, the practice it describes in anything but new and has been shaping the world for centuries. The 'media' has been used to distort truth, manipulate perception, influence politics, distort financial markets and even change the outcomes of wars. Whilst the tools being used might have changed from plays, pamphlets, newspapers, radio, television and now the internet and social media the danger is still the same. It not just the lie itself but it's the slow, grinding corrosion that follows, as trust drains away, societies harden into rival camps, and the very notion of a shared truth begins to look like a quaint relic of a more innocent time.

Back to the story that opened this chapter. It's clear that there are a few things we can learn from the story. Firstly, there can be huge amounts of money in lies and rumours. People aren't (typically) creating fake news for the fun of it, they have a motivation and normally this has some financial element to it. Secondly, the speed that news can travel, even in such a low-tech world as the 19th century. In the story the impact was measurable in days, now days we are talking about hours and minutes.

Fake News

◇ ◇ ◇

In 2014, an investigation into the Veterans Health Administration (VHA) in the USA revealed that staff at several facilities manipulated scheduling data to meet performance metrics and receive bonuses. Patients experienced significant delays in receiving care, and some suffered adverse health outcomes due to postponed treatments. On paper, America's veterans were enjoying record-breaking access to care. Waiting times were falling, targets were being met, and bonuses were flowing. It was a triumph of modern management. Except, of course, it wasn't. This manipulation created the illusion of shorter wait times, masking the true extent of the delays and undermining the healthcare system's mission.

Investigators eventually discovered what patients already suspected: the numbers were a fiction. Staff at multiple VHA facilities had been quietly massaging scheduling data, shifting appointments off the books, and conjuring up the illusion of efficiency. The incentives were clear enough, hit the targets, pocket the bonuses but the consequences were devastating for the veterans. All the while, the system congratulated itself on its "performance" the veterans were suffering delays in their treatment and in some cases serious harm.

So, what had gone wrong and caused this bureaucratic disaster? Firstly, we have the blatant manipulation of the data. When the numbers matter more than the people behind them, someone will always find a way to make the spreadsheet smile. Secondly, there is weak oversight and governance. A system that trusts its own paperwork more than its patients is begging to be deceived. Thirdly, we have a warped set of incentives. If you tie bonuses to wait-time metrics only then you haven't got shorter waits, instead you have creative accounting.

You would think these lessons were obvious. Yet we relearn them, painfully, every few years. Data integrity isn't a technical nicety; it's the foundation of public trust. Incentives must reward real outcomes, not bureaucratic theatre. And oversight must be relentless, because systems left to their own devices tend to drift towards self-preservation, not public service. The VHA scandal is a case study in how bad data doesn't just distort dashboards, it actually has a real-world impact, and in this case hurts people. [4]

◇ ◇ ◇

Augustus Caesar was the name of the first and, by most accounts, greatest Roman emperor. Born Gaius Octavius Thurinus, Octavius was adopted by his great-uncle Julius Caesar taking his name Gaius Julius Caesar in the process. The Senate, in 27 BCE awarded him the honorific Augustus ("the illustrious one"), and he was then known as Gaius Julius Caesar Augustus.

Tensions steadily escalated between Octavian and his former ally, now adversary, Mark Antony. While Antony had relocated to Egypt to live with his lover Queen Cleopatra, Octavian stayed in Rome, cultivating his influence and strengthening his bond with the Roman people. Their rivalry had simmered for about a decade, but public opinion finally turned decisively against Antony after the emergence of a controversial document, Mark Antony's will. This document has huge controversy surrounding it and it's still a matter of debate amongst scholars as to its authenticity.

Octavian read the document aloud in the Senate to the shock of those present. It gave the impression that Mark Antony was betraying Rome for the love of Cleopatra. This all played on anti-eastern prejudice and public suspicion of powerful women by the Romans. To drive home this propaganda Octavian spread copies of the will across Rome and circulated small coins and poetry that painted Mark Antony as a drunk, and therefore, unfit to rule. After defeating him in the court of public opinion he eventually did defeat Mark Antony in battle and went on to rule Rome for over four decades. [2] [5]

The fact that people remember Cleopatra today as the power-hungry temptress that corrupted Mark Antony instead of a shrewd political leader who wanted to protect her crown and maintain her country's independence is a testament to the staying power of Octavian's propaganda.

Next, I want to take you back to the turn of the century, 2001 to be precise, and to a scandal that shook the corporate world to its core. Enron, once one of the most powerful and admired companies on the planet, was an American energy, commodities, and services giant headquartered in Houston, Texas. It was also the epicentre of one of the most jaw-dropping episodes of financial misconduct in modern history.

From internal whistleblowers raising the alarm to the infamous shredding of documents by Enron's external auditors, it soon became clear that much of the data presented to shareholders was, in effect, fiction. The financial statements and annual reports delivered by Enron's executives, and signed off by their auditing firm, were riddled with falsehoods. What investors and the Board of Directors believed to be solid, audited numbers were in reality a carefully constructed façade.

Had Enron's external auditors acted ethically and independently, the fraud might never have reached such catastrophic proportions. The fallout was so severe that it prompted sweeping legislative reform. The Sarbanes–Oxley Act of 2002 was introduced in direct response to the scandal, establishing stricter rules on auditor independence, corporate responsibility, financial disclosures, conflicts of interest, and the overall oversight of public companies.

◇ ◇ ◇

It's worth pausing before we end this chapter to recognise that false data isn't only the work of corrupt companies or criminal fraudsters. Ordinary, law-abiding people contribute to it too. Privacy concerns and unwanted marketing are the leading reasons consumers give inaccurate information online. Research shows that 60% of people intentionally provide incorrect details when asked for their personal data. Birth dates are the most commonly falsified: almost a quarter of consumers admit to giving the wrong date of birth some of the time, 9% do so most of the time, and 5% always enter a false one. [6]

The pattern extends across other data points. Nearly a third of people sometimes use a fake email address or a made-up name, and many also provide incorrect home addresses, phone numbers, job titles, or company names. Given that the immediate consequence of sharing your email is often a surge in targeted advertising and spam, this behaviour is hardly surprising.

But the impact is significant. It only takes a relatively small proportion of 'dirty' entries for a database's value to decline disproportionately. This should act as a wakeup call that even well-intentioned systems can be quietly undermined by the people they rely on.

6. Ambiguous

There is a fantastic BBC comedy skit (which can be found on YouTube [1]), called the Blackberry sketch that features two famous British comedians; Ronny Corbet and Harry Enfield. The scene shows Ronny Corbet going into a grocery shop and asking for help with his blackberry. The whole story line is based around the ambiguity and multiple uses words can have. Some examples from the sketch include Blackberry (mobile phone brand vs fruit), Orange (mobile phone company vs the fruit) and Xbox 360 (the Microsoft games console vs a box of 6 eggs costing £3.60p).

This clever comedy sketch is a homage to the famous Four candle sketch that was originally broadcast on the 18th September 1976 on 'The Two Ronnies' BBC comedy show. The comedy is created through the ingenious use of word play and Homonyms. It centres around a shop keeper (played by Ronnie Corbett) getting frustrated by a customer (played by Ronnie Barker), due to the confusion and misunderstand created by the way the customer speaks.

The scene is set in a hardware store and starts with the shopkeeper (Corbett) handing a lady customer a roll of toilet paper as she is leaving, saying "mind how you go". This throwaway line is a reference to the BBC series Porridge which was a sitcom about a prison and its inmates written by Dick Clement and Ian La Frenais, and also starring Barker.

Into the shop walks a new customer (Barker) who proceeds to ask for what sounds like "four candles". The shopkeeper finds four candles but the customer just repeats his request until it becomes obvious to both of them that there is a miscommunication. At this point the customers rephrase his request as "fork andles, andles for forks" what is actually being asked for are garden fork handles. This skit goes on in this vein as they work through the customers shopping list. For example, another piece of wordplay centres around the word 'plugs', with the customer after bath plugs and the shopkeeper thinking he is asking for electrical plugs.

There are a few things at work in these two sketches. Firstly, we have a general misunderstanding of speech, this might be due to lack of diction, mumbling, language barriers, accents etc. Secondly, we have the ambiguous use of language, or words that have multiple meanings and due to the context (the word is used in) the meaning becomes unclear. The term for this is Homonyms; words that are spelt or sound the same but have different meanings.

Homonyms come in two forms: Homographs and Homophones. Homographs are words that have the same spelling, regardless of how they sound. Examples include: park (park my car and walk in the park), rose (flower and past tense of rising), row (propel with oars and argument and a linear arrangement of seating). Homophones are words that share the same pronunciation, regardless of how they are spelled. If they are spelled the same then they are also homographs. Examples include to, too, two, and there, their, they're and read (peruse) and reed (waterside plant).

It's not only comedians that enjoy utilising this ambiguity, journalists do to. Here are some examples of newspaper articles sourced from Bucknell University [2]:

- British Left Waffles on Falkland Islands
- Dr. Ruth to Talk about Sex with Newspaper Editors
- Lung Cancer in Women Mushrooms
- Teacher Strikes Idle Kids
- Stud Tires Out
- Soviet Virgin Lands Short of Goal Again
- Shot Off Woman's Leg Helps Nicklaus to 66
- Enraged Cow Injures Farmer with Axe
- Miners Refuse to Work after Death

This is all very interesting but why is this so important in the world of data?

The design of a typical IT system has at its foundation a database containing loads of data. This data isn't just dumped all in one big pile but organised and structured so that it can efficiently support the system it is part of and all the other systems and the business users. When the data structure is designed it is based upon the designers and software engineers understanding of the specific pieces of data. The problem comes when different teams create different systems and don't have the same understanding of the data. The following text is taken from my first ever book 'the enterprise data model'. [3]

An example of this is when, a number of years ago, I worked with a major European insurance company and was trying to create a data structure to represent insurance risk. To make it even more complex, the challenge was to model risk across their general, life and health insurance business streams. I wrote about this experience in my first book 'The Enterprise Data Model' and here is an extract:

Initially there was a lot of scepticism especially because risk was considered an easy subject that didn't require any time with the business - IT could handle it. Secondly it was thought impossible to be able to build a model that worked across all three business streams. You can imagine the political hot house that ensued

The first meeting was with the general insurance team who started by telling me how risk was a simple problem to understand. "Everyone in the company understands it so why are we having this meeting" I was told. After some debate we sketched out a high level model showing risk as the central entity and the key entities it interacted with. I then asked the person to my left to expand on the entity 'risk' and provide me with a further level of detail. Within minutes of this conversation, the next person along was interrupting and before long the others in the room also jumped in with different views about different aspects. I then sat and watched the so called experts in risk spend the next thirty minutes arguing over how to define and decompose this single entity. At this point I must admit that I had earlier had similar discussions with the IT guy's so this argument wasn't a huge surprise at all.

What eventually became clear, after further workshops and meetings, was that it is possible to model risk data across all three business streams (life, general and health). The issues were more to do with real understanding of what the data actually means, political protectionism and vocabulary differences.

If I had a pound or dollar for every time I've found two different systems within the same company that represent the same data slightly differently, I would be travelling around the world in a 120m, 7 level super yacht just like Bill Gates. Some typical examples of where you see this problem is with names, addresses and phone numbers.

Let's start with name, how on earth can this be misunderstood? If we imagined, we had three different IT systems all containing the names of individuals but designed by three completely silo'd teams we might have the following:

In system 'A' the capture the name of an individual in a single data field called 'Full Name'. In system 'B' we have the name being captured as two fields 'First Name' and 'Family Name', and in System 'C' we have the fields 'Title', 'First Name' and 'Surname'. This means that we could have the following:

System A:

Ambiguous

- Full Name: 'John Smith'

System B

- First Name: 'John'
- Family Name: 'Smith'

System C

- Title: 'Mr'
- First Name: 'John'
- Surname: 'Smith'

This means that if I want to copy data from System A to System B I would need the computer to understand which part of the name is the first name and which is the Family Name.

Another example would be addresses:

- System A has a single field to store the full address called 'Address'.
- System B has the address broken down into separate lines but the lines have no specific meaning -1st Line, 2nd line, 3rd line, 4th line, 5th line.
- System C has the address broken down into its constituent parts with Building Number, Street, Town, District, Country, ZIP/Postcode.

The examples above are intentionally simple. Sure, modern AI could breeze through them, but that's not really the point. They're there to help the reader get their head around the ideas without dragging in industry-specific jargon or the quirks of a particular organisation. They're just a few illustrations of how different kinds of data might show up and be stored inside a company's systems.

Why does this matter? In chapter 2, Square Peg, Round Hole, we looked at the Ariane rocket that blew up just seconds after take-off. The European Space Agency's investigation found that the disaster came down to a simple but catastrophic mismatch: two parts of the guidance system were effectively speaking different mathematical languages. One used 64-bit numbers and the other used 16-bit. That mismatch represents the digital equivalent of forcing a square peg into a round hole with the resulting errors tearing the rocket apart.

In the corporate world, problems like this crop up all the time, and the fallout can be surprisingly wide-ranging. One of the most common places to see this kind of problem is in the reports and dashboards organisations rely on to make decisions. It's almost a running joke how often management meetings get derailed by debates over whose numbers are "right". When systems don't line up, people end up arguing about data instead of acting on it.

7. The Corporate Data Swamp

The smell of decay hits you first as you see the rotting blackened trees reaching out from the scummy water and boggy land. The whiff of rotting vegetation in the thick stagnant air, moss hanging from branches, and trees that had collapsed into the dank waters of the swamp, decaying in the scum and covered in slimy algae and rot. Welcome to the corporate data swamp!

We like to imagine that large companies have their data neatly under control. After all, they manage to send us a relentless stream of marketing emails that bury the messages we actually care about, so surely, they must have everything sorted! The truth is far less polished as many organisations are wading through their own corporate data swamps, struggling to reach the valuable assets submerged within. All the issues we've explored in earlier chapters apply just as much, if not more, to large enterprises. In fact, there are a few areas where the corporate world seems particularly gifted at getting things spectacularly wrong.

In a 2022 survey undertaken by the polling company Pollfish, they found that 91% of respondents believed their organisation suffered from the impact of data quality at some level. [1] [2] The survey was carried out for the open-source platform Great Expectations and based upon responses from 500 respondents across the US. The type of impact experienced from these data problems where:

- Production delay or product launch delay
- Broken reports and dashboards
- Disagreements over metrics
- Lost transactions
- Business decisions made using incorrect data

This is not a lone set of findings as another survey, by Deloitte this time, showed that more than 67% of executives say they are "not comfortable" in using data from the companies' analytical systems. In a third survey, by KPMG, 67% of CEOs said they prefer to make decisions based on their own intuition and experience due to lack of confidence in the organisation's own insight. [3]

The shocking reality these surveys uncover is that executives have a lack of confidence in the data being provided to them through their own company's information systems. This trust deficit is further evidenced in a survey undertaken in 2022 by the Analytics company SAS. They found that that 42% of analysts and data scientist were having their work being ignored by executives when making decisions. [4]

Trust is one of the most crucial ingredients in the data world. Not only must the data be correct, it must be seen and believed to be correct. For an organisation to make strong, confident decisions it is critical that the data being used to underpin it is understood and trusted.

This is not a new problem. Organisations have been complaining about a lack of confidence in the data they are using for ever it seems. Back in 2004 Forrester Research conducted a survey in conjunction with the Data Warehouse Institute of IT developers, managers and executives. They found that 30% of the them indicated that data quality problems were serious enough to require or attract the attention of the executive function.[5]

So why does this happen and why is it such a never-ending problem? We have obviously already looked at a great many examples of how data quality issues sneak into our world but let's look at a few of the factors that seem to 'shine' the larger the organisation. Just for clarity when I say shine I don't mean it in a positive way.

First, you can build the most immaculate systems known to man, but customers will still find a way to turn everything upside down. In any large residential customer base, roughly 2% of your records will be out of date within a month. Two per cent! Not because the database is failing, but because people are. They move house, switch jobs, tie the knot, untie it again, and, on occasion, exit the stage altogether. The real-world refuses to sit still, and even the cleverest corporate machinery struggles to keep up.

In the business-to-business world, the same headaches apply but often with extra complications. The people you deal with in other organisation don't stay put; they leave, they marry (and change their names), they climb the career ladder or are shuffled sideways into some newly invented role and that's before you get to the companies themselves. Firms restructure, retreat from markets, merge into new ones, launch new products or on occasions go bust and vanish altogether. The corporate landscape is in constant motion, and your data has to keep up. However gleaming the technology, a certain level of error will seep into any organisation's datasets over time. It's not sabotage or incompetence, it's just the inevitable drift of real life, forever refusing to behave as neatly as the systems built to contain it.

Next, we have to be aware of system changes that occur in the data owning organisation. It's not uncommon for upgrades to existing systems or the introduction of new systems can alter, in some way, the existing data. These changes could be in the way that users go about entering data resulting in small but potentially impactful changes. Examples might be the change of units of measure, decimal points, the breakdown of an existing data field into smaller parts (address, name etc). Migrating data from an old system to the latest shiny new system creates the opportunity for errors to creep in. And lastly, we have issued caused by different systems not understand each other well enough. We have given examples early in this book of rockets crashing because two components worked with different units of measure, well this type of problem (and many more like them) also occur in the corporate world.

Many challenges arise due to various factors, such as data inconsistency, incompleteness, and errors during data collection or processing. Addressing Veracity involves employing sophisticated validation, verification, and cleaning techniques to enhance data accuracy.

Many organisations end up with systems that technically contain the same data but interpret it in completely different ways. This typically comes about due to a form of siloed mentality when designing new or modify old systems. There is this view that if I focus on the job at hand and avoid the bureaucracy, I will be able to deliver on time and to budget. Maybe the issue here is expectations management? One platform, for example, might treat an address as four distinct fields; street, town, region, and postcode while another, stores it as a single unstructured blob. The result is predictable, with mismatches, confusion, and endless manual work to reconcile what should have been consistent from the start.

They also fail to defend their data at the point of entry. Without basic validation, bad data slips in and quietly contaminates everything downstream. Take email addresses. A handful of simple checks would stop the majority of invalid entries, whether accidental typos or deliberate junk, from ever reaching a customer record. Ensuring an email contains an '@' symbol, includes something on both sides of it, and ends with a sensible top-level domain would eliminate a surprising amount of noise. And for anyone who hasn't spent their life thinking about this stuff (including the author, until writing this chapter), the top-level domain (TLD for short) is the final part of an email address after the last dot. Familiar examples include '.com', '.net', '.org', '.uk', and '.de'.

The next horror to surface from the Data Swamp is the End User Computing solution or EUC as it is more typically referred to as. In large organisations they have access to highly sophisticated and highly professional system. At least this is what you would assume, but the reality can at times be far from this fantasy world. One of the biggest culprits in this EUC world is the humble spreadsheet.

A spreadsheet is a digital grid made up of rows and columns, designed to organise information, perform calculations, and analyse data. Each intersection, known as a cell, can hold numbers, text, or formulas that automatically update when the underlying data changes. This simple structure makes spreadsheets incredibly flexible: they can function as calculators, databases, modelling tools, budgeting sheets, or dashboards. Modern spreadsheet programs also bundle multiple sheets into a single "workbook," allowing users to structure complex projects across several linked tables.

The idea, however, predates computers by centuries. Early accountants used paper "spreads" laid across desks, literally sheets spread out, to track finances. The leap to electronic spreadsheets came in 1979 with VisiCalc, the first widely adopted digital version, which transformed business computing by automating recalculations that once took hours. This was followed by Lotus 1-2-3 in the 1980s and eventually Microsoft Excel, which became the dominant tool as personal computers spread. These innovations turned the spreadsheet from a digital ledger into one of the most influential pieces of software ever created, shaping everything from corporate finance to personal budgeting.

But it's this very flexibility that becomes a danger for corporations. Spreadsheets let anyone build anything, in any way they like, with no guardrails and no shared standards. What starts as a quick fix or a clever workaround can quietly evolve into a mission-critical artefact that no one fully understands. Over time, organisations accumulate thousands of these bespoke creations each with its own logic, assumptions, and hidden fragilities until the spreadsheet estate becomes a shadow IT system running the business from the sidelines.

In 2012, JP Morgan, one of the world's most sophisticated banks, suffered a $6.2 billion trading loss due to a spreadsheet. Not high-frequency algorithms, or quantum-powered hedge funds, not even a rogue trader with a taste for adrenaline. JP Morgan, a bank with the GDP of a medium-sized nation, discovered that its London office had been managing risk with a tangle of spreadsheets so fragile they made a Jenga tower look like the Hoover Dam. Copy-and-paste, broken formulas and a model that added where it was meant to average. It was less "risk management system" and more "Year 9 ICT project". Yet this was the foundation on which the bank's senior executives confidently assured regulators that everything was under control.

A series of derivative transactions involving credit default swaps (CDS) had been entered by the London unit, reportedly as part of the bank's "hedging" strategy. Trader Bruno Iksil, who became known as the London Whale, had accumulated large CDS positions. An estimated trading loss of US$2 billion was announced, however it was eventually uncovered that the bank had lost more than US$6 billion. [6]

The internal report reads like farce. Risk officers, armed with charts and metrics, believed the bank's exposure was half what it actually was. Half. Imagine driving a car where the speedometer shows 30mph while you're hurtling down the motorway at 70. That's essentially what JP Morgan was doing except with billions of dollars and the global financial system sat in the passenger seat. It's the oldest story in finance: when the data tells you what you want to hear, no one checks the wiring.

In the autumn of 2020, as the UK braced for a second wave of Covid-19, a quiet drama was unfolding inside Public Health England's (PHE). It didn't involve scientists in hazmat suits or ministers at podiums, instead something far more mundane was involved, a spreadsheet.

Every day, labs from across the country sent their Covid test results to PHE. The labs sent clean files of data, neatly structured and ready to be uploaded. PHE on the other hand loaded these files into a spreadsheet. But not any spreadsheet, one from the late 80's which was only able to hold 65,536 rows of data.

For eight days, from 25 September to 2 October, thousands of positive results vanished into the digital ether. On 5 October, Matt Hancock stood in the House of Commons and called it a "legacy system." He wasn't wrong, but the phrase barely captured the absurdity of running a pandemic response on a spreadsheet format old enough to remember the Berlin Wall. By 1am on the 3rd October the problem had been resolved but the damage had been done. For days, half the people who should have been contacted weren't. Infection curves were distorted. And the public, watching the daily case numbers suddenly spike by nearly 23,000, wondered how something so basic could go so wrong. [7]

8. Data Decay

Back in 500BC, the Greek philosopher Heraclitus of Ephesus said "Change is the only constant in life", he goes on to say that "No man ever steps into the same river twice." What he means by this quote is that whilst the river is there and has a name the water in it is continuously flowing and therefore from one second to the next the river is constantly changing.

Just like Heraclitus's river, data is also in a constant state of flux and over time these changes can impact its quality. For example, it is generally considered that approximately 2% of customer records become obsolete in just one month. This data deterioration occurs because customers die, get divorced, marry, and move house. [1] The challenge of data and the impact of time on its quality is encapsulated in three concepts: data decay, data entropy, and data drift.

A customer has moved address but you don't update your customer record, so the next time we try and make contact with said customer, we fail. According to Neil Lucey of Marketscan, customer data can deteriorate at a rate of up to 40% per year. *'Consider how often you see someone on your LinkedIn network celebrating a new position—weekly, perhaps even daily.*' If you're running a business on out-of-date information, it is a recipe for missed opportunities and consequentially diminished revenue. [2]

Data Decay

The average person in Britain moves home every 22.7 years, according to figures published in 2017 from property website Zoopla. Back in 1988 the frequency was much higher with the average of every 9 years.

As you look across the United Kingdom different regions have different rates of change with Scotland being the most frequent at 19.6 years and Wales being home to the longest stayers at 26.8 years. [3] Tenants move even more than home owners. London, for example, has over 1 million privately rented properties with tenants vacating on average every 2.5 years. [4] In the US the combined rate of property moving for a person is on average 11.7 times in their lifetime. [5]

In a 2002 survey by The Direct Marketing Association (DMA) they found that one in three people are changing their email addresses once per year. The reasons behind this might be a change in ISP provider, switching jobs or an attempt to confuse and evade email marketing organisations. In the same survey they also found that the average person has three email addresses, for example personal, work and ISP.

Phone are just as bad according to a survey undertaken by the PhoneArena website. Their results seemed to indicate that 23% of us change our phone number more than once per year, 32% each year and the remaining 45% change our number once every 2 or more years. [6]

The truth is that data changes overtime quite naturally. The harsh reality for businesses trying to use this data is that personal data, as shown above, degrades faster than most. Just think for a moment the impact this change has on direct-to-consumer businesses when this data is used for key activities such as lead generation, customer support and service. This data behaviour is called Data Decay. It simply refers to the gradual loss of accuracy of data over time, due to the normal changes that naturally occur.

Data Entropy

Data Entropy comes from the world of information theory and was introduced to the world in the 1940s by C. E. Shannon. In essence it refers to the level of uncertainty or unpredictability in the data. A high level of randomness to the data means we have a high entropy score and a low randomness gives the opposite result.

Whilst interesting from a statistical point of view, why does this matter? Imagine for a moment a company selling goods though a call centre. When a new customer phones up to buy something from us the call centre agent captures some details about them; such as how they heard about us. If we have a very low Entropy score, because over 80% of the answers for this question are 'Advertising', this can point in two quite different directions. On one hand, it may indicate that an advertising campaign is performing exceptionally well and genuinely dominating customer awareness. On the other, it could signal a process issue in the call centre, where agents may not be asking the question as intended and are instead defaulting to the first option in the dropdown menu. In practice, the data alone can't distinguish between these possibilities, so the pattern should be treated as a prompt to investigate both the effectiveness of the campaign and the integrity of the data collection process.

If we had given the call centre agent an empty field on a screen to fill out instead of a drop-down list, we might find that a low Entropy score actually means that most call centre agents haven't put anything in the field at all, or if the field is mandatory, they have done something like putting a dot in the field. In effect the data in the field has become of little value either due to default values being provided way more than they should or a lack of data at all. It can also indicate that there is something wrong with the data in this field through some kind of system corruption.

A high level of entropy, by contrast, suggests that the data contains a great deal of noise or a large number of outliers. In practical terms, this often means that responses to the question of how customers heard about our company or product are so widely dispersed across categories that the dataset becomes difficult to interpret. When the distribution is this fragmented, it becomes almost impossible to extract meaningful trends or identify dominant acquisition channels, because the signal is effectively drowned out by the sheer variety of answers.

Both AI models and traditional analytical methods, whether charts, tables, or dashboards, struggle to extract meaningful insight from either of these extreme scenarios. To help explain this imagine, for one moment, you're the Director of Marketing of a large business and you're presented with a chart showing that 99% of all sales supposedly came from Advertising, with the remaining 1% spread thinly across every other acquisition channel. Alternatively, picture the opposite: a chart with a hundred different categories, each contributing only a tiny fraction of customer responses about how they heard about your product. In both cases, the data becomes practically useless. The first scenario is so skewed that it raises more suspicion than insight, and the second is so fragmented that no clear trend can emerge. Unless advertising genuinely has become your entire go-to-market strategy, which would be unusual, neither distribution gives you anything reliable to act on.

In customer-facing environments, this makes entropy especially powerful. A sudden drop in entropy might indicate that agents have stopped following the script, that a new interface is nudging them toward a default option, or that customers are being funnelled through a single channel in a way that wasn't intended. A sudden rise, meanwhile, could reflect confusion, inconsistent messaging, or a breakdown in categorisation. In both cases, entropy acts as a diagnostic tool: it highlights when the pattern of responses no longer reflects the underlying reality you think you're measuring.

Data Drift

Now let's go back to 500BC and Heraclitus with his free-flowing river. The water flows smoothly down the river course until something changes, such as a tree falling into the river caused by a lightning strike from a recent storm. This change in the environment, i.e. the tree falling into the river, causes the river to change course. It is just the same with data as the data changes courses due to changes in the environment that you didn't understand or predict. This fundamentally undermines any models or decision making that relies upon this data. Just imagine the effect this would have on a highly sophisticated machine-learning model built to predict when fruit or vegetables might spoil during transport from Spain to Belgium while stored in a specific type of container. The model has been developed on one set of training data but when deployed into the real world we find that the training data doesn't match how the real-world works. This could result in a horrid, smelly and mushy mess.

Machine learning models are trained on historical data, but once they are deployed into the real world, they can lose their accuracy over time and perform differently than expected, this is what we referred to as drift. This can happen for many different reasons. Take the recent COVID pandemic, for example: it didn't just disrupt how the world operated during the height of the outbreak, it also reshaped behaviours and expectations long after the immediate crisis had passed. If we had a model that predicted transport needs at different times of the day based upon pre-COVID commuter patterns and apply that to today's world, post-COVID, we would find the world quite different that pre-COVID and our model would in all likelihood fail.

Another example might be that your machine learning model has been training to detect emails that are spam. Using historical data to enable the model to understand and detect spam email could make it vulnerable to changes in the way spammers use email to trick people. If the types of spam emails that get sent to your inbox change markedly then the AI model will become redundant, as it will not be able to accurately detect that an email is in fact spam.

What about consumer purchasing behaviour? Trends in fashion fluctuate all the time and this will inevitably impact on buying trends and behaviours, for example, changes in home decor, clothing, colour palettes, fair trade, plant based, organic etc. Generational differences compound this with generation X becoming generation Y, becoming eventually generation Alpha and then Beta. Changes in discretionary spending habits often mirror economic conditions, with customers spending more freely in prosperous periods and cutting back during recessions. Ultimately data drift can be caused by changes in the data due to behaviour, external events, or even how the data is actually captured. [6]

The effects of Data Decay, Drift and Entropy aren't immediate but instead build up over time, and if not detected and addresses early can slowly erode the reliability and value of AI and more traditional analysis tools. It is reported that Microsoft estimates that the loss of accuracy within just a single year can be up to 40%. [7]

9. Bad Data Costs!

"... Every year, poor data quality costs organizations an average $12.9 million. Apart from the immediate impact on revenue, over the long-term, poor-quality data increases the complexity of data ecosystems and leads to poor decision making ..." [1]

The above quote is part of research from the analyst company Gartner. The article goes on to say that there is a direct correlation between data quality and organisational performance. They claim that the quality of decision making improves, better sales leads, better understanding of customers and improved relationships with customers. In effect, data is seen by many businesses as a competitive advantage.

"A straw poll of wealth managers conducted by DCI found costs charged to the P&L due to bad data (for client compensation, regulatory fines, etc.) range from 54bps to 111bps of turnover, with an average of 80bps." [2]

Bad Data Costs!

DCI (Data Compliance & Integrity Ltd) is a company that helps investment management businesses with their data quality. So, let's translate their finding into non-financial speak. A basis point is a unit of measure used in finance to describe changes in interest rates, yields, or other percentages. One basis point = 0.01% (one hundredth of a percent). Therefore, what their findings are saying is that between 0.54% to 1.11% of a company's revenues (according to the wealth managers) was being lost due to bad data. This gives us an average of 0.8%.

"…research by Royal Mail Data Services revealed that organisations believe inaccurate customer data costs them, on average, six per cent of their annual revenues. Perhaps more worryingly, over a third were not sure how much it costs them." [3]

This quote chimes with Gartner's own research which found that nearly 60% of companies it surveyed didn't know how much bad data costs their businesses, as data quality wasn't being measured.

"Our studies in cost analysis show that between 15 percent to greater than 20 percent of a companies' operating revenue is spent doing things to get around or fix data quality issues," [4]

the financial cost of poor data quality is $15 million per banking firm. [5]

A 2016 IBM study delivered an even blunter warning: shoddy data isn't just an internal nuisance, it's a macro-economic drag. IBM estimated that poor data quality wipes $3.1 trillion off the U.S. economy every year. The losses show up everywhere from sluggish productivity to system outages and ballooning maintenance bills. It's a reminder that bad data doesn't stay in the back office, it can hit the bottom line of an entire nation.

Although varied in the scale of impact, industry and some of the quotes being quite old, the core sentiment overall is spot on. Bad data costs one way or another, even if you don't realise it is. Just think of the impact this can have on the sales or customer care teams? Time wasted trying to get in contact with customers when their email or phone number are wrong. These types of roles are typically time poor and have to focus their efforts on the best opportunities. This means time wasted on phantom customers is not only time wasted trying to get hold of them but also time that wasn't spent speaking to a customer/prospect that could buy from you. By phantom customer we could be talking about a duplicate record so you waste time, as well as looking stupid, contacting the client a second time.

A recent study by Dun & Bradstreet, the data analytics company, found that one in five businesses have lost a customer because they were relying on inaccurate or incomplete information. Whilst painful in any industry some sectors, such as financial services, where the lifetime value of customers is high and the cost of acquisition is also high will feel the impact the most.

Even if arguments for the value of data quality seems logical, many companies have a hard time justifying the cost of solving it. According to industry analyst Gartner, Inc., about half of enterprises with a CRM (Customer Relationship Management) strategy are unaware of data quality problems. The remainder, however, recognises data quality problems but do not see the value of fixing them (Gartner, 2001). It would not be unfair to say the organisations that disregard data quality and fail to invest are effectively mortgaging their future. They are just pushing the cost to their business down the road.

So, the obvious question to ask is how much does it cost an organisation to disregard the quality of their data? To get a rough ballpark figure we can use the numbers called out in the above research on this topic. Based upon this previous research we have a range of cost estimates

- 0.8% of revenue
- 6% of revenue
- 17.5% of operating revenue (The average of 15% and 20%)

Now these numbers are not exactly comparable. Operating revenue refers only to income generated from a company's core business activities. Revenue on the other hand has a broader meaning, as it includes other income streams. Still, they will serve for an extremely rough and ready estimate. We also have quite different businesses being surveyed and therefore what classes as revenue can be quite different.

If we calculate the average of the three numbers we have, we end up with a figure of 8.1% of revenue. Before a wave of emails arrives telling me that "revenue is vanity, profit is sanity," or pointing out that you could drive a bus through my calculation, let me say this: the point isn't precision, it's perspective. My bringing together these numbers and my school boy calculation we get a sense of the scale of impact.

 To further illustrate this, we can look at the potential impact on the wider economy. For example, the combined total revenue of all companies listed on the New York Stock Exchange (NYSE) in 2024 is estimated at around $60 trillion (TTM) across roughly 2,100 listed firms. If you follow the logic further, we can estimate that the revenue of these companies could be increased by circa $4.86 trillion.

That's enough about research on this topic, what about real world actual examples? News stories about data quality problems are hard to come by as organisations don't really like to launder there dirty washing in public. But I've collected together a few examples that did reach the news.

The airline industry, for example, has frequent issues with bad data. It causes both extra costs which impact business profitability but it also can have a major PR impact. The problem of mistaken fares, for example, is so bad that some experts go searching for these mistakes to alert their followers. The errors that trigger these mistaken fares can come from a variety of sources; human error, currency mix-ups and software glitches.

In 2018 British Airways cancelled thousands of passenger tickets due to an incorrect fare being offered. This issue occurred on the 11th June between 17:45 and 11:00 the following day. It seems that flights to Tel Aviv and Dubai which normally retailed at over £200 were selling for £1 plus airport taxes.

The impact was tangible (financial), and intangible (brand sentiment). Not only did BA have to stomach the costs involved in the administration effort required to cancelling all the incorrectly booked flights. It wouldn't have been insignificant to issue all those refunds and the compensation vouchers of £100. The effect on the company's reputation is a lot harder to measure. Based upon the reaction on notice boards and in the news, it was clear that the £100 compensation did little to dampen down the anger in its customers that their tickets where not being honoured. Some customers didn't even find out about this error until they checked their online BA account. [6]

This example is not an isolated incident, according to Thrifty Nomads which tracks these kinds of mistakes and based upon a quick search on the internet I find the following examples:

- 2007: San Francisco → Auckland, NZ (Return, Business Class): $1,500 instead of $15,000. Cause: a missed zero.
- 2012: Myanmar → US (Return): $300. Cause: currency conversion mistake.

- 2013: US cities → Hawaii (Return): $7. Cause: 2-hour computer glitch.
- United Airlines: Business Class: $79 instead of $4,000. Cause: Danish Kroner ↔ British Pound conversion error.
- Cathay Pacific: First Class Vietnam → US: $1,000 instead of $16,000. Cause: mispricing.
- Qatar Airways: Business Class Vietnam → US: $750 roundtrip. Cause: pricing error.
- Delta Airlines – Premium Economy to Europe: $600. Cause: glitch.
- Lufthansa: Business Class to Europe: $1,000 instead of $4,000. Cause: mispricing.
- Various US Airlines: Hawaii roundtrip: $7. Cause: system glitch.

[7] [8] [9]

In an article in the May 2017 issue of PC Mag the journalist Tom Brant had a story about Uber and approximately $50M of its drivers' money that it hadn't paid out. It seems that for years Uber had been calculating the earning of drivers in New York based upon an incorrect formula. He explains that instead of collecting its 25% commission after tax and fees, the company was actually taking this money before tax and fees had been subtracted. This meant that drivers had been over charged by circa $50 million. The refund that the drivers where owed, if you include interest, would amount to an average of $900 per driver. [10]

Back in the early 2000's I used to run my own boutique data consultancy business. On one memorable day I popping into a major office supplies superstore to purchase a printer. I'll not mention the companies name but they are a global concern. During the process of buying the printer I signed up for a business account. My logic was that I assumed over the next few years it would be advantageous as I was likely to buy further equipment in the future. Many months went by and to be honest I'd forgotten all about the account I'd opened with them. Then imagine my surprise when 6 months later a letter arrives from the retailer, welcoming me to my new business account and providing me with a set of vouchers to spend on more stuff. The only problem was that the vouchers where 3 months out of date!

The letter had a number of issues with it:

1. The name on the account was wrong. They had my name down as 'Andy Grahay'.
2. The postcode was incorrect 'OXT' not 'OXY'.
3. Lastly and most disturbingly the letter actually had two street in the address. The first street was 'Bluethroat Close' and this was followed by 'Cormorant Place'. At the time I used to live in Cormorant Place and still to this day have no idea where Bluethroat Close was.

I actually tried to reach out to the organisations CIO as I couldn't believe what they had done, but to no avail. Suffice to say I never did use that retailer again.

We can see from the above stories that bad data can have a hard financial impact on an organisation. We know data is a strategic asset and that it can have a financial cost but how much? It can be difficult for organisations to understand how to prioritise and understand how important, questions such as:

- What tangible and measurable benefit will I get from this project?
- What will data quality management cost?
- What's the impact to my organisation?

The best place to start is by using an easy-to-understand example from the direct marketing world. If we take a simple example of a global enterprise which we will call 'ABC plc'. The company has built a contact database of 500,000 individuals, a prized asset that has taken significant time and investment to assemble. Now assume that 10% of those records contain an incorrect email address. That could mean a malformed address (perhaps missing a domain), an inbox that no longer exists, or an address that's actively blocked. Each of these issues will trigger either a hard or soft bounce.

If we further assume that the conversation rate for a campaign is 3% (typical conversation rates are between 2-5% so this would seem a good average to go with). The cost of running a single campaign we can estimate as £20,000 and we have a product that we are selling for £25. So, this gives us:

A	Cost of email Marketing Campaign	£20,000
B	Number of Contacts emailed	500,000
C	Conversion rate	3%
D	% of incorrect emails	10%
E	No of incorrect emails	50,000

Based on these numbers, we can compare the marketing campaign against the same campaign but run with perfect data. This will enable us to understand the impact that data quality has had on the business's income. When compared we get a difference of £37,500. The breakdown is as follows:

		With incorrect email addresses	With correct email addresses
F	Number of contacts actually contacted (B-E)	450,000	500,000
G	Number of Sales (F*C)	13,500	15,000
H	Revenue Generated (G*£25)	£337,500	£375,000
I	Net Revenue (H-A)	£317,500	£355,000

This means that the lack of investment in improving the companies' data quality has cost the business £37,500 for just a single marketing campaign. If the company runs say 10 campaigns in a year the annual cost of data quality rises to £375k.

Our second example is a call centre situation. A good customer experience for both the company and customer is one that takes place smoothly, accurately, and most importantly, quickly. In a recent article, Siebel estimated that the cost to handle a single customer service call can range from $300 to $350, based on the length of the call, the company's infrastructure, training costs, peak times, downtime, personnel, and facilities needed to handle the call.

Better data quality can improve the financial performance of the call centre by:

- Faster response times for customer requests, since customer service representatives can more quickly find correct customer information. Representatives spend less time correcting records.
- Reduced costs of buying the product, since a complete customer profile is available to representatives. Reps can handle more calls, allowing management to staff fewer people in the call centre.
- More responsive technical support staff that can access customer's histories and the histories of other customers with the same product.
- Better understanding of buying patterns that allows representatives to better manage the sales process and ensure high conversion ratios.
- Stronger capabilities for up sell and cross sell. Business intelligence applications armed with more accurate data can accurately indicate customer profiles that are historically receptive to similar sales efforts.

Every second you can shave off call centre interactions, saves you money. Over the course of a single year, even a two-second time saving per phone call could add hundreds of thousands of dollars to the bottom line.

A	Cost per second per agent in call centre	£0.5
B	Seconds lost due to data quality issues per call	2 sec
C	No of calls an agent will complete on average every hour	20
D	No of Agents in the call centre	2,000
E	Number of working days a year for an agent	220

F	Number of Seconds lost to data quality in a day (B*C*8 hour working day)	320 sec
G	Number of seconds lost per year (F*E)	70,400 sec
H	Annual cost of data quality per agent (G*A)	£35,200
I	Total cost per annum for all agents in the call centre (H*D)	£70,400,000

So very quickly we reach some quite staggering numbers. In this example we end up with a cost for the data quality problems over the course of a single year as being over £70 million.

When we return to my opening estimate of $4.86 trillion in lost value across the US economy, derived from 2024 NYSE figures, it no longer reads like a provocative exaggeration. By this point in this book, the scale of the problem has revealed itself: fragmented data, inconsistent definitions, operational drag, and the compounding effect of thousands of small inefficiencies across millions of daily decisions.

Seen through that lens, the potential 8.1% uplift in revenue and profit available to organisations that get data quality right becomes far easier to grasp. It is not a fantasy number. It is the logical outcome of removing friction from processes, restoring trust in information, and enabling people to act with clarity rather than hesitation.

The real message is simple: data quality is not a technical hygiene issue. It is one of the largest untapped sources of economic value available to modern organisations. And the price of ignoring it is already being paid; quietly, continuously, and at staggering scale.

10. Intangible

"The intangible represents the real power of the universe. It is the seed of the tangible."

Bruce Lee [1]

"Value is not always visible. Sometimes, it's invisible and intangible."

Pooja Agnihotri [2]

In the 1920s and 30s most companies had a significant investment in tangible assets such as property, physical products, raw materials, etc. Since the 1980s this has been gradually changing as more intangible assets (such as intellectual property, marketing brands, IT systems and the data that resides in them) have made up the true value of companies. This can be illustrated by looking at the average market to book ratio for companies in the 1980s (just over 1) to today where according to the S&P it is 4.9 (as at 12th March 2025). A market-to-book ratio of 4.9 implies that the tangible assets of an average US business account for approximately 20% of the value of the company. Put another way it means that investors value the companies on the S&P at 4.9 times what they are worth on their accounting books. This means that they would pay $4.9 for every $1 of net assets (assets minus liabilities). In essence intangible assets have supplanted tangible assets as the key value drivers in today's economy.

During the same period traditional accounting has remained tied to tangible assets. As a result, a significant portion of corporate assets go under recognised and under reported. Because it is difficult and some would say impossible to manage what is not being measured, many of the assets that are most responsible for creating value in today's economy are not managed, as well as they could be.

The reverse is therefore also true in that intangibles that drive up the value of companies can equally drive the value down. The corrosive impact of bad data, for example, also has costs which are hard to quantify. Flawed data breeds customer distrust, undermines regulatory compliance, and erodes reputational capital. It hampers innovation, stalls digital transformations, and weakens the adoption of artificial intelligence. Perhaps most insidiously, it blinds organisations to their own effectiveness, leaving leaders unable to judge whether resources are being deployed wisely.

A recent study on the lack of trust around data found that 91% of IT decision-makers believe they need to improve the quality of data in their organizations, yet 77% admit they don't fully trust the data they already have. [3] According to another survey of CFO's this time it showed that nearly 89% of CFOs believe they are making decisions based on inaccurate or incomplete data on a monthly basis. [4]

We discussed in the previous chapter the financial cost of bad data but I would argue most of the impact is hard to quantify in pounds, dollar, euro's or yen terms. There is a great book I read many years ago by Baruch Lev called 'Intangibles'. Lev is a finance person so looks at the topic from an accountant's perspective. His thesis goes like this.

Modern financial statements are fundamentally broken because they fail to capture the true drivers of corporate value: intangibles such as data, software, brands, R&D, customer relationships, organisational know-how, and human capital. Because accounting rules treat most intangibles as expenses rather than assets, Lev says:

- Companies look far less profitable than they actually are
- Investors are flying blind
- Managers are incentivised to under-invest in the very things that create long-term value
- Market volatility increases because reported numbers don't reflect economic reality

In short, he is arguing that the global economy has shifted to intangible value creation, but accounting has not.

◇◇◇

When organisations can't guarantee that customer data is accurate, complete, and up to date, their exposure to regulatory risk rises sharply. Many industries, such as healthcare and finance, are bound by strict regulations concerning data accuracy and privacy. Compliance frameworks across industries, from HIPAA to the Sarbanes-Oxley Act (SOX) and the Gramm-Leach-Bliley Act, all have a dependence on one foundational requirement, that the data is accurate, secure, and well-governed. Finally, under Europe's GDPR (General Data Protection Regulation), companies have obligations to have accurate and up-to-date personal data.

Many enterprises continue to struggle with this regulatory data nightmare. Without confidence that customer records are correct, companies face a heightened risk of non-compliance, which can lead to significant fines, operational disruption, or reputational damage.

Accurate data also strengthens internal controls. SOX Section 404, for example, requires organisations to disclose material risks. Something as simple as an incorrect customer address can trigger a cascade of issues, for example misdirected invoices, delayed payments, bad debt, and ultimately misstated financial results. These seemingly small data errors can become compliance failures.

◇◇◇

Trust is the first casualty of unreliable data. When teams encounter conflicting reports, inconsistent metrics, or unexplained discrepancies, confidence in the organisation's information assets deteriorates.

This mistrust doesn't remain confined to data; it spreads into processes, systems, and even leadership decisions. Over time, the organisation becomes hesitant, second-guessing insights that should be routine. This results in:

- Impaired Decision-Making: Strategic and operational decisions rely on a stable foundation of facts. Poor data veracity introduces uncertainty into that foundation, forcing leaders to make choices based on incomplete or misleading information. Whether forecasting demand, allocating resources, or evaluating performance, decision-makers are left navigating through ambiguity rather than clarity.
- Lowered Predictability and Weakened Forecasting: Predictive models and forecasting tools are only as strong as the data that feeds them. When data is inaccurate or inconsistent, predictive accuracy declines. This leads to unreliable forecasts, unexpected variances, and a diminished ability to anticipate market shifts or operational risks. Organisations lose the ability to plan proactively and instead find themselves reacting to avoidable surprises.
- Inconsistent Management Reporting: Management reports are intended to provide a single, authoritative view of performance. Poor data veracity fractures that view. Different systems produce different answers to the same question, and reconciliation becomes a manual, time-consuming exercise. Instead of enabling insight, reporting becomes a

negotiation or in reality an argument over who's numbers can be trusted.

Building Trust and Organisational Credibility: Data-driven insights are routinely shared with investors, regulators, partners, and customers. The credibility of those insights depends entirely on the integrity of the underlying data. When veracity is strong, stakeholders trust the organisation's narrative. When it is weak, confidence erodes quickly. Veracious data strengthens the organisation's reputation, reinforcing its commitment to transparency, accuracy, and sound governance.

◇◇◇

In the end, the value of data is inseparable from its accuracy. High-quality, trustworthy information is the gateway to meaningful insight; when veracity slips, analysis becomes distortion. Organisations increasingly lean on analytics to guide transformation, but without reliable inputs, even the most sophisticated models simply amplify noise. Reliable data strengthens decision-making, enabling leaders to act with confidence—whether they're interpreting customer behaviour, optimising operations, or anticipating market shifts. The same principle extends beyond business: public policy, social programmes, and community-level interventions all depend on accurate demographic, economic, and health data. When the facts are wrong, the consequences ripple far beyond balance sheets.

The cost of poor-quality or outdated data is rarely dramatic in the moment, but it is relentless. Missed opportunities, wasted resources, reputational damage, and misguided strategic bets accumulate quietly until they become impossible to ignore. A marketing team targeting an audience that moved on two years ago is not an edge case—it's the everyday reality of data decay. And for organisations that pride themselves on being data-driven, this creates a profound dilemma: the more you rely on data, the more exposed you are when that data is wrong. In a world where intangible assets increasingly define competitive advantage, the integrity of your information isn't just a technical concern. It is the foundation on which all other value is built.

Customer experience: In industries like e-commerce and social media, understanding customer behaviour is vital. Accurate data about customer preferences, purchasing patterns, and feedback is crucial for personalised marketing and enhancing user experience. Veracity in customer data ensures that businesses can tailor their offerings to meet customer expectations accurately.

Predictive Analytics: Reliable historical data is used to predict future trends and behaviours. Inaccurate data can lead to flawed predictions, impacting businesses' ability to anticipate market changes and customer preferences.

Brand reputation: Veracity ensures that the data shared with the public and media is accurate. A piece of inaccurate information can tarnish a company's reputation. Reliable data builds brand credibility and trust, enhancing the organisation's image in the eyes of the public and potential investors.

11. The River of Bytes

"The Nile River flows over 6,800 kilometers (4,000 miles) before emptying into the Mediterranean Sea. For thousands of years, the river has provided a source of irrigation to transform the dry area around it into lush agricultural land. Today, the river continues to be a vital freshwater resource for millions of northeast Africans who rely on it for irrigation, drinking water, fishing, and hydroelectric power."

National Geographic [1]

The source of a river marks the geographical point where its journey begins. Its typically found in elevated areas such as mountains, hillsides, glaciers, or natural springs. Places where rainfall, snowmelt, or groundwater first gathers and can be channelled into a continuous stream. This starting point is commonly called the headwaters, origin, or upstream.

At the river's source, if you were mindful to, it would be easy to spot and remove pollutants like mud or debris. Like the small plastic carrier bag (the type used to store vegetables when doing your weekly supermarket shop) that gets dropped onto the hillside by a careless hiker, walking in the alpine mountains. It falls by the small trickling stream, dropped by mistake (or intent) after consuming a snack. The next day we have rain which washes the bag down the stream to enter the midstream stage of the river.

The rivers midstream, or middle course, is the next stage of the rivers journey. The river has now matured beyond its youthful, steep beginnings but hasn't yet reached its wide, slow-moving lower course. We find the river flowing more smoothly down gentler slopes. The river has eroded its banks creating a broader channel that curves and bends downstream. Now that a number of tributaries have joined the river, the volume of water it is carrying has increased considerable.

As the river flows, pollutants mix and spread. Our plastic bag has floated downstream and is breaking apart, contaminating the water by spreading itself across the full breadth of the river. Whilst it's quite easy to remove the bag upstream, we now need to start using nets, boats and way more manpower. Cleaning up midstream can even require efforts such as filtration plants, dredging, or chemical treatments.

Finally, our plastic bag reaches the delta, the point where the river meets the sea. This final stage in the rivers travels is called the lower course. It's where the river ends by eventually flows into another body of water; such as the sea, ocean or potentially another river. By now the bag has been smashed and dashed into millions of small pieces. At this stage the river is at its widest and deepest with far lower energy levels. As the bag disintegrates into microplastics it is now almost impossible to remove from the river. The downstream impact of the plastic bag is catastrophic, as it is poisoning the fish and polluting the rivers ecosystem. The effort involved in removing the bag from the river is now immense, especially if you compare it to the minimal effort that was required to prevent the litter entering the river at source.

In the data world it's the same. Data quality is not so different in its nature to the way that rivers are formed. We start with little pockets of errors get into the organisations data ecosystem, just like the tributaries described above. These travel through the data ecosystem until they have infected everywhere.

Fixing errors early is far less costly than dealing with them later. G. Loabovitz and Y. Chang defined a data management rule to capture this concept which they called the 1:10:100 rule. The key principle behind this theory is that fixing defects or problems has an escalating cost depending on the stage in the process in which it gets resolved. The earlier a quality problem is identified, the cheaper it will be to fix.

Identifying a data issue at source typically costs around 1% of what it will cost to fix once that same bad data has propagated across an entire IT ecosystem. It's far cheaper to implement basic data validation, such as checking the contents of an email field, than to wait until incorrect data has been entered, replicated, and embedded in downstream systems.

For example, validating an email address at the point of entry isn't difficult. At minimum, you can check that it contains the essential components: a username, an '@', and a domain name that includes both a mail server ('gmail', 'yahoo', etc.) and a top-level domain ('.com', '.co.uk', and so on). If you're feeling more ambitious, you can even ping the address to confirm it actually exists.

By the time you're fixing data issues midstream, you're already spending £10 for every £1 you could have spent preventing them. Once errors surface in reports, dashboards, or operational systems, the cost to correct them is typically an order of magnitude higher than if fixed at source. This isn't just the cost of the technical fix, but of the total business cost.

Take a CRM system with poor quality email data. If a significant proportion of its email addresses are invalid, incomplete, or simply wrong, then a large share of outbound communications will bounce or fail. That means wasted marketing spend, inaccurate engagement metrics, lost revenue opportunities and the operational drag of repeatedly cleaning up the email addresses.

Finally, we get to the downstream stage which in data terms is when the data quality issue has spread across the entire organisations IT landscape. To prevent irreversible damage to the organisation through the impact to customers or business decision making we need to spend £100 for every £1 we would have spent preventing the bad data occurring in the first place. This represents lost revenue, reputational harm or even regulatory penalties.

It is important to recognise that the 1:10:100 ratios are illustrative rather than precise. These figures are meant to convey the exponential increase in costs associated with data errors, which can vary depending on organisational size, industry, and specific circumstances. Nonetheless, the underlying principle of exponential cost growth remains consistent across contexts.

So, we can see that using the river analogy works well in explaining how fresh, clean water, is similar to data in that it is a critical shared resource that requires careful stewardship. Protecting data at its source ensures that downstream processes and systems benefit from high-quality information. The 1:10:100 rule encapsulates this principle, emphasising that small, proactive investments in data quality can prevent significantly larger issues later. This rule underscores the importance of preventative measures over corrective actions, highlighting that early intervention is more cost-effective and efficient.

Equifax is a great example of the 1:10:100 rule. Over a three-week period between March and April 2022, the company incorrectly assessed millions of consumers credit rating. The impact on those individuals, who's credit score was out by 20+ points in some cases, was that their applications for car loans, mortgages, and credit cards were either rejects or the interest rate was raised.

It seems that somewhere down the river, probably in the mid-stream, we have a series of calculation that were fundamentally flawed. Examples were given such as the "number of inquiries within one month" or the "age of the oldest tradeline". The whole sordid situation was exposed by the Wall Street Journal which caused the company's share price to dive 5%. Shortly after this the company was hit with a class action lawsuit. The real price of Equifax's three-week data crisis won't be clear until the class action lawsuit concludes. [2]

◊◊◊

AS we have discussed in this chapter, data quality behaves like a river system. Whatever enters at the source will inevitably flow downstream, gathering cost, complexity, and consequence as it goes. The further bad data travels, the more expensive it becomes to correct. That is the essence of the 1:10:100 rule; a pound spent on prevention can spare ten on correction and a hundred on remediation.

Upstream controls such as validation rules, thoughtful interface design and user training are the equivalent of installing light, inexpensive defences at the riverbanks. A small mesh net at the source keeps the entire waterway clean. Neglect those measures, and you're effectively allowing pollution to drift unchecked, expecting downstream teams, systems, and customers to absorb the damage. Errors compound, risks multiply, and costs escalate in ways that are entirely predictable and entirely avoidable.

The cheapest place to fix data is always at the point of origin, everything else is just managing the consequences.

12. Ghosts in the Machine

Doom has come upon you, upon you who dwell in the land. The time has come! The day is near! There is panic, not joy, on the mountains.

Ezekiel 7:7

"There have always been ghosts in the machine. Random segments of code, that have grouped together to form unexpected protocols. Unanticipated, these free radicals engender questions of free will, creativity, and even the nature of what we might call the soul."

I, Robot (2004)

Just picture for a moment a beautiful sunny Sunday morning. You have a lovely steaming cup of coffee to blow away those slowly fading cobwebs of sleep, whilst you flick through your various news feeds and notifications on your mobile phone. As your mulling over the contents of your digital device, you suddenly get the overwhelming urge to search for your own name and see what the world says about you. To scratch this itch, you load up Google, Bing (or whatever is your search engine of choice) and type in the letters of your name, one by one. The need to satisfy your curiosity is intense as your one keystroke away from sliding into the digital rabbit hole, a shadowy oubliette where curiosity and vanity collide.

If you've had this urge of curiosity you're not alone. A 2022 survey by BrandYourself revealed that 60% of Americans have Googled themselves, while nearly a third admit to doing it at least once a month. [1]

So, what is behind this compulsion? What motivates an individual to search for their online presence and reputation? According to another survey on this subject by ReputationDefender in 2019, there are a number of reasons for this behaviour ranging from just simple curiosity to the monitoring for identify theft.

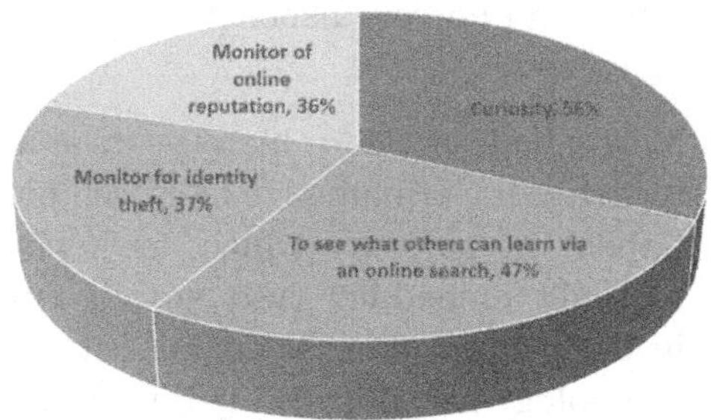

top reasons people search for their own name

But it's not only searching for their own name that people are obsessed with. A study by Pew Research in 2016 found that 56% of us had looked up someone else's name. The key reasons given for this were:

- To find someone they have lost touch with (53%)
- To learn more about someone they met socially (51%)
- To learn more about a prospective date (41%)
- To learn more about a neighbour (29%)
- To learn more about a prospective employee (29%)

So, imagine for a moment the German journalist Martin Bernklau who, in a moment of curiosity hit that search key. He expected the usual LinkedIn profile, maybe an old picture of himself from university, some little morsel of a breadcrumb from his digital life. But instead, the search engine stares back at him with the shocking news that he is a child abuser, an escaped mental patient and a fraudster! [2] [3] As you would expect Bernklau was hit with a mixture of horror, disbelief and shock. How had this happened?

Martin had served for many years as a criminal court reporter in Germany. He had been using Microsoft's Copilot AI software which, as is common now, is typically embedded into search engines or used instead as a search engine. It seems that the technology had mistakenly linked him to the crimes of Fritz Haarmann, one of Germany's most infamous mass murderers. The AI algorithm had discovered a blog that Bernklau had published where he discussed the play 'Totmacher'. Deathmaker, which translates into German as 'Der Totmacher', is a 1995 film directed by Romuald Karmakar based on the police interviews with Fritz Haarmann, a notorious serial killer at the time. Copilot, it seems, had falsely identified him as the author of the play and by association of the crimes outlined within it.

Bernklau said while the case affects him personally, it should also be a matter of concern for other journalists, legal professionals, and really anyone whose name appears on the internet. Bernklau has subsequently hired a lawyer and proceeded to sue Microsoft for defamation and invasion of privacy as the organisation responsible. It should be noted for balance that Copilot's terms of service disclaim responsibility.

This story shows how AI is not full proof and can provide incorrect results. Just like a human it can make mistakes, producing answers that are not only wrong, but at times disturbingly convincing. These AI generated errors have become known as hallucinations. The term is loosely analogous with human hallucinations but rather than being an issue of perception (as with a human) it is the result of erroneously constructed content. For example, an AI powered chatbot may include random falsehoods which can seem quite plausible, especially when delivered with the air of authority that these software agents typically use. This issue has not gone unrecognised with research showing that chatbots hallucinate as much as 27% of the time [4] and that factual inaccuracies can be found in up to 46% of generated texts. [5]

AI has been with us since the 1950's, but really hit the public conscience with the launch of software such as Chat GPT, Google's Bard and Microsoft's CoPilot in the early 2020's. This type of technology has a fundamental symbiotic relationship with data. In essence, AI requires huge amounts of data which it uses as a knowledge asset to mine for the answers to the questions and problems it is tasked with. It works not by finding discrete answers from the data, but by understanding the world through the experience that is portrayed in the data. This means that when its making decisions, they are based upon its learnt knowledge from the data assets it has consumed. It should be obvious that the quality of the data is critical, as it directly impacts on the reliability of the model. AI is only as good as the data its consumed.

Visualise yourself sitting in your autonomous car as it carries you steadily down the motorway at 70 miles an hour. Just imagine for a moment what might happen if the cars brain is using data with some errors in it! The outcome could potentially be devastating.

Just as with humans, AI has the ability to learn through natural evolution. With humans we learn by making mistakes, such as touching a flame which burns our finger. We store this knowledge in our brain so that next time we are confronted with a flame we don't touch it. AI is no different and this trait is behind some of the issues called out above. In 1995, Stephen Thaler had proved how an AI model hallucination emerges from its neural networks through the random perturbation of their connection weights. [6]

So, what does that all mean? In essence, small random values can be added to the weighting given within the AI model. This prevents the model getting stuck with a good set of weighting but not the best set of weightings. Imagine just nudging the weightings by a little to enable the model to find a better set of weightings and hence better results. So, in effect a minuscule level of chance is added to enable the AI to not get stuck with the same bland answer every time, but instead to learn and evolve.

In 2022 ChatGPT burst into the world's consciousness. It heralded the rise of a generation of AI technology called Generative AI. ChatGPT was (and at time of writing still is) only one of a wave of AI software such as Microsoft Copilot or Google's Gemini. We see companies throwing huge amounts of money at this type of AI in a drive to grow their businesses and cut costs through the removal of staff.

This type of software generates new content based upon the material it has ingested. Therefore, the quality of the content ingested (or data, as that is what the documents and websites its ingested really are) has a massive impact on the quality of its output. Welcome to the well-worn phrase from the good old days of IT called Garbage In/Garbage Out (GIGO). To reenforce this further it was found in a recent study by Bloomberg, that 11 leading Generative AI models, including GPT-4o, Claude-3.5-Sonnet, and Llama-3-8 B, would produce bad results if given one of 5,000 harmful prompts. [7]

In July 2021, Meta (then Facebook) launched BlenderBot 2, a conversational AI engine that used the internet to supplement its knowledge base. During the release Meta mentioned that the system is prone to "confident statements that are not true". At the time these hallucinations were framed as a technical limitation rather than a bug. [11] The early ChatGPT release was also well known for embedded plausible sounding but false details in its responses. A study by Vectara, a generative AI startup, found that AI chatbots invented information anywhere from three to 27 per cent of the time. [12] This counter intuitive outcome from their research has huge implications for customer support AI systems and any question answering agent. In fact, as AI seems to be overtaking search this finding has massive consequences for average internet user and AI development teams.

One of the causes of such a problem and an area of growing concern is the AI cannibalism that is now occurring in front of our eyes. Since 2022 we have seen a growing amount of content that has been created by AI. Emails, web pages, reports, studies, student essays and even books (not this one I might add). As the industry rushes towards the moment when human generated content has been exhausted and its only ingesting synthetic content, we reach the moment of AI model collapse. This is the moment when AI starts to eat itself as the AI is consuming content from either itself or other agents. This leads us right back to GIGO.

The new breed of AI software is able to pull information from other data sources than those it has been training on. This reduces hallucinations and improves the responses...BUT. Over the last few years more and more of the content accessible via the web (articles, blogs, images, web sites, etc) has been generated using AI. Whether the creation of this synthetic content using AI is due to laziness or efficiency the harsh reality is that AI is now training itself more and more using content created by other AI system.

"We've now exhausted basically the cumulative sum of human knowledge ... in AI training,"

Elon Musk

In January 2025, Elon Musk told an audience during a livestreamed conversation with Stagwell chairman Mark Penn, that there's little real-world data left to train AI models on. [8] There seems to be three fundamental issues in the AI generated doom loop.

Firstly, we have the concept of 'Hallucination Accumulation'. This is where the errors generated through the AI models hallucinations build up over time as models inherit the errors of previous models which in turn amplifies the errors. This causes content to drift slowly away from the original truths.

Secondly, we have the loss of exceptions within our data. This is where rare data points are removed from the content, leading to the gradual obscuring of entire concepts.

Thirdly, and finally, we have the potential for narrow patterns to get repeated and re-used repetitively. This creates a biased understanding from the reader or content consumer that the idea is common rather than atypical and potentially bizarre. We see this today with social media feeding users with more and more of the content they have accessed, creating a world view that enhances the prevalence of the content being pushed on the user. In effect AI can be responsible for the reinforcement of narrow viewpoints or patterns as though they are common and obvious recommendations.

These scenarios occur because of errors that get compounded across iterations of models leading to distortion in the responses. The AI models are trained on their own AI generated content which leads to a gradual loss of accuracy and the introduction of bias. In the world of AI this phenonium has become known as AI model collapse.

We're going to invest more and more in AI, right up to the point that model collapse hits hard and AI answers are so bad even a brain-dead CEO can't ignore it.

Steven J. Vaughan-Nichols [9]

So maybe the fear that all those white-collar jobs will be gobbled up by AI is wrong. Maybe Generative AI underpinned by a LLM is not the long-term answer? Scientist and writer Gary Marcus states the simple reality that *"There are too many white-collar jobs were getting the right answer actually matters."* [10]

13. Data's Dimensionality

So, we have reached the final chapter of this book and we have journeyed through an interesting aspect of the data landscape. The mismatched records, the fat fingers, the crashed space craft, the duplicated customer, the systems that insist someone is a child abuser and an escaped mental patient. After a while, you start to realise that the real mystery isn't why these things happen, but how on earth we're supposed to make sense of them.

I want to change tack a little and instead of more stories about data misbehaving, let's step back and ask a more fundamental question: how do we even begin to understand the behaviour of our data in the first place? As we have seen by the various stories, a large part of the problems we have encountered are issues with the technology. So, the obviously place to start seems to be with how technologists look at data quality, and as you would expect they have an answer to this. They always do! And while it's not perfect, it gives us a way to look at data not as a chaotic mess but as something we can observe, classify, and, with a bit of luck, improve.

In the world of data management, the idea of "good" or "bad" data isn't, always just left to gut feeling. Instead, some organisations use something called data quality dimensions. This is a set of characteristics that help us judge whether the data is "fit for purpose." Just think of them as the behavioural traits of data: the things we can measure, track, and hold it accountable for.

There's no single canonical list. Google will happily offer you six, seven, eight, or ten dimensions depending on who you ask. But they all circle the same themes. For simplicity, let's borrow the version used by DAMA International, the global association that sets many of the standards data professionals quietly rely on every day. DAMA define six data quality dimensions, which are:

- Accuracy: Accuracy is the most basic question of all: is this true? Does the name match the person? Does the weight match the product? If your system insists someone weighs 2 kg, you don't need a PhD in data science to know something has gone wrong.
- Completeness: Completeness is about whether the data you need is actually there. You can't run an email campaign without email addresses. You can't allocate hospital beds if half the records don't include the ward. And crucially, a complete dataset can still be completely wrong — fullness is not the same as truth.
- Uniqueness: Uniqueness deals with the ghosts and doppelgängers of the data world. Two records may look different — different

addresses, different phone numbers — yet still refer to the same person. In healthcare, this isn't just inconvenient; it's dangerous. Critical information gets marooned in the "other" record, unseen by the people who need it most.

- Consistency: Consistency is the quiet killer of trust. When one system says you were born in 1984 and another insists it was 1986, people stop believing either. Consistency is less about correctness and more about coherence — the sense that the organisation knows what it knows.
- Timeliness: Timeliness is about freshness. Some data spoils quickly — bed availability in a hospital, for example. Other data ages more gracefully — quarterly figures, demographic trends. But all data decays eventually. During the pandemic, timeliness wasn't a luxury; it was the difference between responsive care and blind decision-making.
- Validity: Validity is the bouncer at the door. It checks whether the data even looks right: Does the email contain an "@"? Is the month between 1 and 12? Is the date actually a date? Validity doesn't guarantee truth, but it stops the most obvious nonsense from getting in.

Once organisations adopt these dimensions, they often build dashboards of KPIs (Key Performance Indicators) to track how their data behaves over time. These dashboards don't fix anything by themselves, but they do something more important: they make the invisible visible. Suddenly, "our data is terrible" becomes "email completeness is 62% and falling." And once you can see a problem, you can do something about it.

But even this framework doesn't tell the whole story. Two broader ideas sit above all the dimensions: Trust and Impact. Trust is the emotional residue of data quality. It's what people feel when the data behaves predictably, or doesn't. Trust isn't built by perfection; it's built by reliability. Impact on the other hand asks the most human question of all: what happens if this is wrong? A misspelled name is irritating, but a duplicated patient record could be catastrophic. Impact helps organisations prioritise what to fix first, because not all errors are created equal.

Data quality is multidimensional because trust itself is multidimensional. When organisations use these dimensions, they move beyond vague complaints and into a world where data can be assessed, understood, and improved. And in doing so, they unlock something powerful: the ability to treat data not as a liability to be feared, but as a strategic asset that behaves, more often than not, in the way we need it to.

14. Final Words

So, here we are at the end of this book with our final chapter designed to tie off the arguments, tidy the loose threads, and spare the superstitious amongst us from ending on a chapter 13. What have we learned? As the title of this book calls out, data will behave badly if we let it. It is slippery, stubborn, and occasionally spiteful.

Like politicians and teenagers, data has the knack of misbehaving at the worst possible moment. You can pour money into platforms, dashboards, and consultants in smart suits, yet a single rogue spreadsheet can still bring your world crashing down around your ears. Ask anyone who lived through the UK Government's COVID reporting fiasco or JP Morgan's infamous spreadsheet fuelled loss.

For years, corporate executives have been sold the fantasy of immaculate data. Software vendors sell amazing tools that will guarantee the cleanliness of your data whilst consultants sell governance frameworks that ensure your using the tools correctly. But anyone who has worked with data knows that the truth is far different. Data wriggles, mutates, and hides surprises in database columns you didn't know existed. Over the course of the pages of this book, we have learnt that data entry errors can have massive consequences with huge amounts of money, people careers and even the defence of one's country potentially at risk.

Even when the data is correct, it can still cause havoc. We learnt in chapter 3 that perfectly accurate information, misunderstood or stripped of context, can be just as dangerous as bad data. Georgina Sturge's story about how UK immigration figures were being misinterpreted, and therefore the government under estimated the level of migration that had been occurring, shows this. We also explored how surveys and statistics can be made to give you the answer you want. Remember Sir Humphrey Appleby and the way he ran rings around a survey on national service.

We have explored the world of AI and how the technology is fundamentally designed to create errors, just like our human brains. The tech bros who dominate the AI world have called these mistakes 'hallucinations' rather than what they really are ... data error!

So, the real challenge with data is not simply "data quality" but understanding the veracity of data; its truthfulness, reliability, and integrity. As our world fills with structured and unstructured data alike, veracity becomes a question of bias, noise, incompleteness, outliers, and errors.

So, what is this book really about? As I mentioned in the opening introduction chapter, the uncomfortable truth with data is that data doesn't always tell the truth. We've long called data "the new oil," but unlike oil it is infinitely replicable, constantly generated, disturbingly easy to contaminate and the consequences can be far worse. In 2022 alone, humanity created or consumed 97 zettabytes of it; by 2025, that number is estimated to be 181 zettabytes. The cover of this book shows a radioactive sign for a good reason. Instead of the oil analogy a better option would be atomic energy. Handled with care, data illuminates and empowers but neglect or misunderstand it and the consequences can be serious and far-reaching.

Welcome to the world of data behaving badly.

References

Introduction

[1] A&E Television Networks, 2015.

[2] Amazon company timeline,

Internet Archive Wayback Machine, Updated: August 2007,

https://web.archive.org/web/20071027122712/http://phx.corporate-ir.net/phoenix.zhtml?c=176060&p=irol-corporateTimeline

[3] Spiro, Josh. "The Great Leaders Series: Jeff Bezos, Founder of Amazon.com".

[4] Amazon Annual Reports 2012, 2013, 2014, 2015

[5] Jeffrey Dastin, Insight - Amazon scraps secret AI recruiting tool that showed bias against women, Reuters, October 11, 2018

https://www.reuters.com/article/world/insight-amazon-scraps-secret-ai-recruiting-tool-that-showed-bias-against-women-idUSKCN1MK0AG/

[5] Mars Climate Orbiter, Mishap Investigation Board, Phase I Report, November 10, 1999,

https://llis.nasa.gov/llis_lib/pdf/1009464main1_0641-mr.pdf

[6] UTC is Coordinated Universal Time, the global time standard that the world uses to keep clocks and time zones aligned. It's maintained using incredibly precise atomic clocks and astronomical observations to keep Earth's rotation and our clocks in sync.

[7] Justin Gray, WSB-TV, Wed 29th March 2023, https://www.yahoo.com/news/city-tears-down-man-atlanta-215228366.html

[8] Definition of Veracity, Collins,

https://www.collinsdictionary.com/dictionary/english/veracity

[9] Veracity, Cambridge University Press and Assessment, https://dictionary.cambridge.org/dictionary/english/veracity

[10] Colby Hopkins, The History of Amazon and its Rise to Success, Michigan Journal of Economics, May 1, 2023,

https://sites.lsa.umich.edu/mje/2023/05/01/the-history-of-amazon-and-its-rise-to-success/

Chapter 1 – Fat Fingers

[1] Chris Witts, To Err Is Human—Forgiveness Is Divine – Part 1 — Morning Devotions, Hope 103.2, 11th January 2024,

References

https://hope1032.com.au/stories/faith/2024/err-human-forgiveness-divine-part-1/

[2] Alexander Pope, Wikipedia,

https://en.wikipedia.org/wiki/Alexander_Pope

[3] Trader made error in 'flash crash', Citigroup says, BBC.com, Published 3 May 2022,

https://www.bbc.com/news/business-61303217

[4] Sara Gates, 5 Examples of Bad Data Quality in Business — And How to Avoid Them, Monte Carlo, Published 27 Sept 2023,

https://www.montecarlodata.com/blog-bad-data-quality-examples/

[5] Reuters, 'Fat finger' error by Samsung Securities results in shares worth S$132b issued to employees, M today, Published 10th April 2018,

https://www.todayonline.com/fat-finger-error-samsung-securities-results-shares-worth-s132b-issued-employees

[6] Kim Na-young, Appellate court upholds conviction of ex-Samsung Securities employees in 'ghost' stock case, Yonhap News Agency, Published 13th August 2020,

https://en.yna.co.kr/view/AEN20200813008400315

[7] Samsung Securities raided over share blunder, DW Business, 05/28/2018,

https://www.dw.com/en/samsung-securities-raided-over-fat-finger-share-issuance/a-43955305

References

[8] (2nd LD) Regulator inspects Samsung Securities over 'fat-finger' dividend chaos, Yonhap News Agency, Published 9 April 2018.

https://en.yna.co.kr/view/AEN20180409010400320

[9] Ju-Min Park, Samsung Securities CEO resigns after $105 billion stock blunder, Reuters, July 27, 2018,

https://www.reuters.com/article/business/samsung-securities-ceo-resigns-after-105-billion-stock-blunder-idUSKBN1KH1AZ/

[10] Sweden GDP - Gross Domestic Product, countryeconomy.com,
https://countryeconomy.com/gdp/sweden?year=2014

[11] Economy of Sweden, Wikipedia, https://en.wikipedia.org/wiki/Economy_of_Sweden

[12] Ebony Bowden, History's biggest 'fat-finger' trading errors, The New Daily, Oct 02, 2014,

https://www.thenewdaily.com.au/finance/finance-news/2014/10/02/historys-biggest-fat-finger-trading-errors

[13] Blake Stilwell, How a Misplaced Decimal Point Nearly Took Down Spain's Newest Submarines, Military.com, April 29, 2021,

https://www.military.com/military-life/how-misplaced-decimal-point-nearly-took-down-spains-newest-submarines.html

References

[14] New Spanish submarine has serious weight problem, El País, 8 May 2013,

https://english.elpais.com/elpais/2013/05/08/inenglish/1368039150_776450.html

[15] Kate Ressler, Bad Math: The Impact of Medication Dosage Miscalculations, Pharmacy Times, 8 June 2020,

https://www.pharmacytimes.com/view/bad-math-the-impact-of-medication-dosage-miscalculations

[16] J.K. Aronson, Medication errors: what they are, how they happen, and how to avoid them, QJM: An International Journal of Medicine, Volume 102, Issue 8, August 2009, Pages 513–521, https://doi.org/10.1093/qjmed/hcp052

[17] Cavell GF & Mandaliya D, Magnitude of error: a review of wrong dose medication incidents reported to a UK hospital voluntary incident reporting system, European Journal of Hospital Pharmacy 2021;28:260-265.

https://ejhp.bmj.com/content/28/5/260

[18] Nicole Villeneuve, 5 of the Most Famous Typos in History, November 2, 2023,

https://historyfacts.com/arts-culture/article/5-of-the-most-famous-typos-in-history/

[19] Rare Bible from 1631 discovered, Good Reading, Feb 2023,

https://goodreadingmagazine.com.au/book-briefs/rare-bible-from-1631-discovered/

[20] Stefan Andrews, The Biggest Typo in Church History Produced the 'Wicked Bible', The Vintage News, Oct 10, 2018,

https://www.thevintagenews.com/2018/10/10/the-wicked-bible/

Chapter 2 - Square Peg, Round Hole

[1] OUR HISTORY Commercial Aircraft, Airbus, Accessed 14/1/2026,

https://mediaassets.airbus.com/pm_38_736_7362 24-9et6bmlkjp.pdf

[2] Clement Charpentreau, The story of Airbus: the genesis of a European giant, AreoTime, 11 October 2022,

https://www.aerotime.aero/articles/32351-the-story-of-airbus-the-genesis-of-a-european-giant

[3] Andrew Curran, How Computer Design Software Delayed The Airbus A380, Simple Flying, 25 Nov 2020,

https://simpleflying.com/airbus-a380-computer-design-delay/

[4] Software discrepancies delayed the Airbus A380, Rubenerd, 5 February 2023,

https://rubenerd.com/software-discrepancies-delayed-the-airbus-a380/

References

[5] Failed Project Series - What Went Wrong with the A380?, Beyond Software Blog,

https://blog.beyondsoftware.com/failed-project-series-what-went-wrong-with-a380

[6] The Chairman of the Board: Prof. J. L. LIONS, ARIANE 5 Flight 501 Failure Report by the Inquiry Board, 19 July 1996,

http://sunnyday.mit.edu/accidents/Ariane5accidentreport.html

[7] 2000: World celebrates New Millennium, BBC, Accessed 6 February 2026,

http://news.bbc.co.uk/onthisday/hi/dates/stories/january/1/newsid_2478000/2478173.stm

[8] Y2K, Smithsonian, Accessed 6 February 2026,

https://www.si.edu/spotlight/y2k

[9] Rajiv Chandrasekaran, Y2K Repair Bill: $100 Billion, Washington Post, 18 November 1999,

https://www.washingtonpost.com/wp-srv/WPcap/1999-11/18/077r-111899-idx.html#:~:text=U.S.%20businesses%20and%20government%20agencies%20are%20being%20forced,the%20most%20expensive%20peacetime%20catastrophe%20in%20modern%20history.

Chapter 3 - Misunderstanding The Data

[1] Keith A. Pickering, The First Voyage of Columbus, columbuslandfall.com, Accessed 6 February 2026, http://columbuslandfall.com/ccnav/v1.shtml

[2] Joshua J. Mark, World History Encyclopaedia, Christopher Columbus, 12 October 2020,

https://www.worldhistory.org/Christopher_Columbus/

[3] Jeffrey B. Russell, Inventing the Flat Earth, Praeger, 1991

[4] R S Benner, "Watch Your Units!" Part 1 – Even Columbus Had Trouble With Units, GlobalSpec, 12 October 2018,

https://cr4.globalspec.com/blogentry/29124/Watch-Your-Units-Part-1-Even-Columbus-Had-Trouble-With-Units

[5] Georgina Sturge, 'Bad Data, How Governments, Politicians and the Rest of Us Get Misled by Numbers', The Bridge Street Press, 2023, chapter 1.

[6] Richard Witkin, JET'S FUEL RAN OUT AFTER METRIC CONVERSION ERRORS, The New York Times Archives, 30 July 1983, Section 1, Page 7

Chapter 4 - Lies, Dam Lies and Statistics

[1] The quote is commonly attributed to Benjamin Disraeli, a British Prime Minister, but it was popularized by Mark Twain in his 1907 autobiography. Twain wrote, "Figures often beguile me, particularly when I have the arranging of them myself; in which case the remark attributed to Disraeli would often apply with justice and force: 'There are three kinds of lies: lies, damned lies, and statistics'".

Velleman, P. F.. Truth Damn Truth and Statistics, Journal of Statistics Education, 16(2), 97, 2008,

https://doi.org/10.1080/10691898.2008.11889565

[2] Yes, Prime Minister, s01e02 Episode Script, The Ministerial Broadcast, 1986,

https://www.springfieldspringfield.co.uk/view_epis ode_scripts.php?tv-show=yes-prime-minister-1986&episode=s01e02

[3] Yes Prime Minister questionnaire design matters, IPSOS, 20.02.24,

https://www.ipsos.com/en-uk/yes-prime-minister-questionnaire-design-matters

[4] Timandra Harkness, John Graunt at 400: Fighting Disease with Numbers, Significance, Volume 17, Issue 4, August 2020, Pages 22–25, https://doi.org/10.1111/1740-9713.01421

References

[5] Andy Graham, A Brief History of Data, 24 Aug. 2024, Koios Publishing

[6] Number of telephones in use and households with radio and television sets in the United States from 1876 to 1986, Statista, Accessed 2 February 2026,

https://www.statista.com/statistics/1247483/us-number-telephones-radio-tv-historical/

[7] 35,028,682 PHONES IN WORLD IN 1936, New York Times, April 26, 1937, Page 21,

https://www.nytimes.com/1937/04/26/archives/35028682-phones-in-world-in-1936-nearly-half-or-17423871-in-use-in.html

[8] Cell Phones by Country 2026, World Population Review, Accessed 2 February 2026,

https://worldpopulationreview.com/country-rankings/cell-phones-by-country

[9] Sharon L. Lohr and J. Michael Brick, Roosevelt Predicted to Win: Revisiting the 1936 Literary Digest Poll, DOI 10.1515/spp-2016-0006

https://gwern.net/doc/statistics/bias/2017-lohr.pdf

[10] Famous Statistical Blunders in History, Emory, Accessed 2 February 2026,

https://mathcenter.oxford.emory.edu/site/math117/historicalBlunders/

[11] Altman D G, Bland J M. Missing data BMJ 2007; 334 :424 doi:10.1136/bmj.38977.682025.2C

https://www.bmj.com/content/334/7590/424

Chapter 5 - Fake News

[1] Boase, G.C.; revised by James Lunt. "Cathcart, Charles Murray, second Earl Cathcart [formerly Lord Greenock] (1783–1859". Oxford Dictionary of National Biography (online ed.). Oxford University Press. doi:10.1093/ref:odnb/4886. (Subscription or UK public library membership required.)

[2] Marinel Mamac, 7 Biggest Fake News Stories in History (And What We Can Learn From Them), A Little Bit Human, 22 February 2022,

https://alittlebithuman.com/7-biggest-fake-news-stories-in-history-and-what-we-can-learn-from-them/

[3] Definition of 'fake news', Collins, Accessed 2 February 2026,

https://www.collinsdictionary.com/dictionary/english/fake-news

[4] CNNHealth, "A fatal wait: Veterans languish and die on a VA hospital's secret list" by Scott Bronstein and Drew Griffin, CNN Investigations, Updated 9:19 PM EDT, Wed April 23, 2014, https://edition.cnn.com/2014/04/23/health/veterans-dying-health-care-delays/

[5] A brief history of fake news, BBC, Accessed 2 February 2026,

https://www.bbc.co.uk/bitesize/articles/zwcgn9q

[6] Mindi Chahal, Consumers are 'dirtying' databases with false details, Marketing Week, 8 Jul 2015,

https://www.marketingweek.com/consumers-are-dirtying-databases-with-false-details/

Chapter 6 - Ambiguous

[1] The One Ronnie (Ronnie Corbett, Harry Enfield), MY BLACKBERRY IS NOT WORKING!, BBC,

http://www.youtube.com/watch?v=6dmhF1rqaZk

[2] NEWSPAPER HEADLINES FOR SYNTAX, Accessed 2 February 2026,

https://www.departments.bucknell.edu/Linguistics/synhead.html

[3] The Enterprise Data Model: A framework for enterprise data architecture, 2nd edition, published 2012

Chapter 7 - The Corporate Data Swamp

[1] Elliot Leavy, Data Quality Crisis: New Survey Reveals 77% of Organizations Have Quality Issues, AI Data & Analytics Network, 28/06/2022,

https://www.aidataanalytics.network/data-governance/articles/data-quality-crisis-new-survey-reveals-77-of-organizations-have-quality-issues

[2] John Russell, Data Quality Study Reveals Business Impacts of Bad Data, Big Data Wire, 17 June 2022,

References

Data Quality Study Reveals Business Impacts of Bad Data

[3] KPMG 2025 CEO Outlook – UK, KPMG, Accessed 2 February 2026,

https://kpmg.com/uk/en/insights/strategy/kpmg-ceo-outlook-uk.html

[4] Analytics leader SAS surveyed data scientists to identify roadblocks to digital transformation

Posted on 14, February 2022 by EuropaWire PR Editors | This entry was posted in Business, Industrial, Science, Technology, United Kingdom and tagged Accelerated Digital Transformation, AI, AI ethics, analytics, data, data scientists, digital transformation, Digital transformation, Dr Iain Brown, Dr Sally Eaves, job dissatisfaction, SAS, survey. Bookmark the permalink.

https://news.europawire.eu/analytics-leader-sas-surveyed-data-scientists-to-identify-roadblocks-to-digital-transformation/eu-press-release/2022/02/14/13/43/24/97460/

[5] Data Warehouse Institute and Forrester Research, 2004

[6] 'London whale' traders charged in US over $6.2bn loss, BBC, 14 August 2013,

https://www.bbc.co.uk/news/business-23692109

[7] Andrea Downey, How using Excel may have caused thousands of unreported Covid cases, DigitalHealth, 8 October 2020.

Chapter 8.   Data Decay

[1] The widely cited figure that 2% of records in a customer file become obsolete every month originates from data quality research and industry analysis, particularly from sources like TDWI (The Data Warehousing Institute) and academic studies on data degradation.

[2] Neil Lucey, The Hidden Cost of Data Decay: Why Keeping Your Customer Records Fresh is Crucial for Business Success, Market Scan, 28th Aug, 2024,

https://www.marketscan.co.uk/insights/the-hidden-cost-of-data-decay/

[3] Brits move home every 23 years, Zoopla, 13 September 2017,

https://www.zoopla.co.uk/press/releases/brits-move-home-every-years/

[4] How Often Do Tenants Move Home? A Look Across the UK, Charles David Casson, 21 February 2025,

https://www.charlesdavidcasson.co.uk/how-often-do-tenants-move-home-a-look-across-the-uk/

[5] Moving Statistics 2025, ConsumerAffairs.com. 14 Mar 2024,

https://www.consumeraffairs.com/movers/moving-statistics.html

[5] Will Sturgeon, How often do you change your email address?, ZD Net, 16 Oct 2002,

https://www.zdnet.com/article/how-often-do-you-change-your-email-address/

[6] Moez Ali, Understanding Data Drift and Model Drift: Drift Detection in Python, Datacamp, Jan 11, 2023,
https://www.datacamp.com/tutorial/understanding-data-drift-model-drift?dc_referrer=https%3A%2F%2Fwww.bing.com%2F

[7] Data Drift: What It Is, Why It Matters, and How to Tackle It, DASCA, 21 March 2025, https://www.dasca.org/world-of-data-science/article/data-drift-what-it-is-why-it-matters-and-how-to-tackle-it

Chapter 9 – Bad Data Costs!

[1] Data Quality: Best Practices for Accurate Insights, Gartner,

https://www.gartner.com/en/data-analytics/topics/data-quality

[2] The hidden cost of bad data, DCI, https://www.wealth-dci.com/wp-content/uploads/2023/01/dci-whitepaper-the_hidden_cost_of_bad_data.pdf

[3] The cost of bad data: have you done the math? - Global Marketing Alliance, https://www.the-gma.com/the-cost-of-bad-data-have-you-done-the-math

References

[4] CIO Magazine - Feb. 15, 2001.

[5] Navin Ahuja, The Hidden Cost: How Poor Data Quality Undermines Financial Decision-Making, Data Risk Fortnightly, 18 May 2025,

https://www.linkedin.com/pulse/hidden-cost-how-poor-data-quality-undermines-financial-navin-ahuja-9d8me/

[6] British Airways cancels 2,000 'incorrectly' cheap tickets, BBC, 20 June 2018,

https://www.bbc.co.uk/news/uk-44546400

[7] Thrifty Nomads,

https://thriftynomads.com/airline-error-mistake-fares-cheap-flights/

[8] United Airlines to honour tickets issued for $0 in glitch, BBC, 14 September 2013,

https://www.bbc.co.uk/news/world-us-canada-24089326

[9] www.thriftytraveler.com

[10] Tom Brant, Oops: Uber Kept Nearly $50M of Drivers' Money, PC Mag, May 24, 2017,

https://uk.pcmag.com/news/89454/oops-uber-kept-nearly-50m-of-drivers-money

Chapter 10 – Intangibles

[1] Bruce Lee. "Bruce Lee Striking Thoughts: Bruce Lee's Wisdom for Daily Living", Tuttle Publishing, 2015, p.74,

[2] Pooja Agnihotri, 17 Reasons Why Businesses Fail :Unscrew Yourself From Business Failure, 9 June 2021

[3] research firm Vanson Bourne (commissioned by SnapLogic)

[4] Adam Zaki, 9 in 10 Finance Leaders Knowingly Making Decisions Off Bad Data, CFO.com, Dec. 6, 2023,

https://www.cfo.com/news/bad-data-bad-planning-pigment-survey/701671/

Chapter 11. The River of Bytes

[1] Nile River, National Geographic,

https://education.nationalgeographic.org/resource/nile-river/

[2] Sara Gates, 5 Examples of Bad Data Quality in Business — And How to Avoid Them, Monte Carlo, Sep 27 2023,

https://www.montecarlodata.com/blog-bad-data-quality-examples/

Chapter 12. AI Hallucination

[1] Shane Barker, What Happens When You Google Your Name? An Inside Look at How People Search and What It Means for Your Online Presence, Expert Beacon, September 24, 2024,

https://expertbeacon.com/what-happens-when-you-google-your-name-an-inside-look-at-how-people-search-and-what-it-means-for-your-online-presence/

[2] David Gerard, Copilot AI calls journalist a child abuser, Microsoft tries to launder responsibility, 23 August 2024,

https://pivot-to-ai.com/2024/08/23/microsoft-tries-to-launder-responsibility-for-copilot-ai-calling-someone-a-child-abuser/

[3] Thomas Claburn, Microsoft Bing Copilot accuses reporter of crimes he covered, The Register, 26 Aug 2024,

https://www.theregister.com/2024/08/26/microsoft_bing_copilot_ai_halluciation/

[4] Metz, Cade (6 November 2023). "Chatbots May 'Hallucinate' More Often Than Many Realize". The New York Times. Archived from the original on 7 December 2023. Retrieved 6 November 2023.

[5] de Wynter, Adrian; Wang, Xun; Sokolov, Alex; Gu, Qilong; Chen, Si-Qing (September 2023). "An evaluation on large language model outputs: Discourse and memorization". Natural Language

Processing Journal. 4 100024. arXiv:2304.08637. doi:10.1016/j.nlp.2023.100024.

[6] Thaler, S.L. (January 1995). "'Virtual input' phenomena within the death of a simple pattern associator". Neural Networks. 8 (1): 55–65. doi:10.1016/0893-6080(94)00065-T.

Ricciardiello, Luciana; Fornaro, Pantaleo (May 2013). "Beyond the cliff of creativity". Medical Hypotheses. 80 (5): 534–543. doi:10.1016/j.mehy.2012.12.018. PMID 23452643.

Thaler, S. L. (2016). "Cycles of insanity and creativity within contemplative neural systems". Medical Hypotheses. 96: 34–43. doi:10.1016/j.mehy.2016.07.010. PMID 27515220.

Thaler, Stephen L. (2014). "Synaptic Perturbation and Consciousness". International Journal of Machine Consciousness. 6 (2). World Scientific Publishing Company: 75–107. doi:10.1142/S1793843014400137.

Thaler, S. L. (Fall 1996). "The Death Dream and Near-Death Darwinism". Journal of Near-Death Studies. 15 (1).

[7] Bloomberg AI Researchers Mitigate Risks of "Unsafe" RAG LLMs and GenAI in Finance, Bloomberg Professional Services, April 28, 2025,

https://www.bloomberg.com/professional/insights/press-announcement/bloomberg-ai-researchers-mitigate-risks-of-unsafe-rag-llms-and-genai-in-finance/

References

[8] Kyle Wiggers, Elon Musk agrees that we've exhausted AI training data, Tech Crunch, 8 January 2025,

https://techcrunch.com/2025/01/08/elon-musk-agrees-that-weve-exhausted-ai-training-data/

[9] Steven J. Vaughan-Nichols, Some signs of AI model collapse begin to reveal themselves, The Register, 27 May 2025,

https://www.theregister.com/2025/05/27/opinion_column_ai_model_collapse/

[10] Andrew Zinin, Generative AI's most prominent skeptic doubles down, Tech Xplore, 29 May 2025,

https://techxplore.com/news/2025-05-generative-ai-prominent-skeptic.html

[11] TOBB AI, The Concern in Today's World: AI and Hallucination, Medium, 14 Aug 2023,

https://medium.com/@tobb_AI/the-concern-in-todays-world-ai-and-hallucination-467ccfd1284b

[12] Chatbots may 'hallucinate' more often than many realise, The Straits Time, 11 Nov 2024,

https://www.straitstimes.com/world/united-states/chatbots-may-hallucinate-more-often-than-many-realise

Index

Index

Index

Acknowledgements

I have spent a significant amount of my corporate career having to deal with data that is misbehaving, wrong, misused or just misunderstood. So, when I came across a half-written book on Big Data that I had tried to write but had abandoned, something must have clicked. Within that book the obvious subject of the 4 Vs of Big Data is discussed, and it occurred to me that the Veracity dimension remains under explored.

After a little research into data quality and into the wider topic of Veracity, convinced me there was more than enough material for the book you're now reading. It's been quite fun in pulling this together and I hope as a reader you enjoy reading the text as much as I did in researching it.

As ever, writing does not happen in isolation. Many people have contributed; some knowingly, others without realising it. First and foremost, my thanks go to my partner, Angela, whose support and belief is unwavering and whose patience as I wrestle with ideas is extraordinary. I'd also like to thank my son Alex for reading an early copy and giving me feedback on it.

Acknowledgement

I am also grateful to the many organisations I've worked with over the years, companies like Rentokil Initial, HSBC, IMS Health, BG Group, BAT, AXA, The Pensions Regulator, Sybase, Hummingbird and Business Objects. The data quality challenges I encountered in these environments have shaped much of my thinking, and I remain indebted to the lessons they provided.

All research for this book was carried out by me alone, and I take full responsibility for any errors that remain.

And finally, if I have inadvertently overlooked anyone who should be acknowledged, please accept my sincere apologies it is an omission of memory, not gratitude.

Andy Graham

East Sussex, 9 April 2026

The Enterprise Data Model: A framework for enterprise data architecture, 2nd edition, published 2012

Mastering Your Data, published 2015

A Brief History of Data: How data has become the worlds new addiction, published 2024